D1302991

HOW
BARACK
OBAMA
FOUGHT THE
WAR ON TERRORISM

John A. Torres

Enslow Publishing
101 W. 23rd Street
Suite 240
New York, NY 10011
USA

enslow.com

Published in 2018 by Enslow Publishing, LLC.
101 W. 23rd Street, Suite 240, New York, NY 10011

Library of Congress Cataloging-in-Publication Data

Names: Torres, John Albert, author.
Title: How Barack Obama fought the War on Terrorism / John A. Torres.
Description: New York : Enslow Publishing, 2018. | Series: Presidents at war
| Includes bibliographical references and index. | Audience: Grades 7-12.
Identifiers: LCCN 2017003129 | ISBN 9780766085350 (library-bound)
Subjects: LCSH: Obama, Barack--Military leadership--Juvenile literature. |
Terrorism--United States--Prevention--Government Policy--Juvenile
literature. | War on Terrorism, 2001-2009--Juvenile literature. | United
States--Military policy--21st century--Juvenile literature. | United
States--Foreign relations--2009---Juvenile literature. | United
States--Politics and government--2009---Juvenile literature.
Classification: LCC HV6432 .T66 2018 | DDC 363.325/160973090512--dc23
LC record available at https://lccn.loc.gov/2017003129

Printed in the United States of America

To Our Readers: We have done our best to make sure all website addresses in this
book were active and appropriate when we went to press. However, the author and
the publisher have no control over and assume no liability for the material available
on those websites or on any websites they may link to. Any comments or suggestions
can be sent by email to customerservice@enslow.com.

Photo Credits: Cover, pp. 1, 5, 8, 19, 29, 39, 49, 59, 69, 80, 90, 100, 109 Peter
Souza/White House; Cover (background) Orlok/Shutterstock.com; p. 4 Spencer
Platt/Getty Images; p. 9 Obama Press Office/Newscom; p. 12 Dorling Kindersley/
Getty Images; p. 15 Alex Wong/Hulton Archive/Getty Images; p. 17 Jewel Samad/
AFP/Getty Images; p. 20 Roberto Schmidt/AFP/Getty Images; p. 26 Mark
Wilson/Getty Images; p. 30 jpa1999/DigitalVision Vectors/Getty Images; p. 33
Canovas Alvaro/Paris Match Archive/Getty Images; p. 35 Maher Attar/Sygma/
Getty Images; p. 41 Georges De Keerle/Hulton Archive/Getty Images; p. 44
Bloomberg/Getty Images; p. 46 The White House/Getty Images; pp. 51, 73 Mario
Tama/Getty Images; p. 53 dapd/AP; p. 56 ullstein bild/Getty Images; p. 60 Lonely
Planet Images/Getty Images; p. 63 Peter Parks/AFP/Getty Images; pp. 66, 75
Pool/Getty Images; p. 71 meshaphoto/E+/Getty Images; p. 78 Ahmad Al-Rubaye/
AFP/Getty Images; p. 82 Mandel Ngan/AFP/Getty Images; p. 85 Boston Globe/
Getty Images; p. 92 Pierre Suu/Getty Images; p. 93 Drew Angerer/Getty Images;
p. 96 Alex Wong/Getty Images; p. 97 U.S. Navy/Getty Images; p. 101 Tasos
Katopodis/AFP/Getty Images; p. 103 Anadolu Agency/Getty Images; p. 107
NurPhoto/Getty Images; p. 110 Science & Society Picture Library/Getty Images;
pp. 112-128 (background) Everett Historical/Shutterstock.com.

CONTENTS

New York's World Trade Center is on fire after two hijacked planes were flown into the two towers on September 11, 2001.

INTRODUCTION

So many countries throughout the world have lived with terror attacks and the threat of terrorism long before that threat and that fear came to the United States on September 11, 2001.

Much like the date of December 7, 1941—when the Japanese attacked American forces at Pearl Harbor, drawing the United States into World War II—the date of September 11 would go down in infamy. The truth is that after December 7, 1941, and September 11, 2001, the country was never the same.

On September 11, 2001, Islamic terrorists hijacked four passenger jets with the intent of flying them into iconic American landmark buildings that would be full of people. That morning two separate jets flew into the two tallest buildings of the World Trade Center, known as the Twin Towers, killing thousands of innocent people who had just arrived at work. A third plane crashed into the Pentagon in Washington, DC, while the fourth jet crashed in an empty field in Pennsylvania after passengers revolted against the terrorist hijackers.

When the smoke cleared and the bodies were counted, the death toll stood at 2,996 with more than 6,000 injured.[1] That death toll actually continues to rise as more people die every year from complications due to injuries suffered during the attacks.

After 9/11 just about every American knew the name Osama bin Laden, the terrorist and mastermind behind the attacks on this nation. The American president at the time of the attacks was George W. Bush, and the American people pressured him to retaliate at once against those who had attacked the United States.

But this was not as simple as President Franklin D. Roosevelt's decision to declare war on Japan after the attack on Pearl Harbor. The terrorists who decided to use airplanes as weapons on that September day were made up of citizens from several different countries. They had no government to speak of or land that they could legitimately call their own.

The war on terrorism would have to begin slowly. The first thing that was needed was a massive emphasis on intelligence to find out where the terrorist leaders were hiding, who was helping, and how they were being funded.

The night of the attacks, Bush went on television to reassure the American people that this new type of war, this war on terrorism, would be won.

"The search is underway for those who were behind these evil acts," Bush told the frightened nation. "I have directed the full resources of our intelligence and law enforcement communities to find those responsible and to bring them to justice. We will make no distinction between the terrorists who committed these acts and those who harbor them."[2]

The war on terrorism continues. It defined not only the presidency of George W. Bush but that of his successor, President Barack Obama.

HUMBLE BEGINNINGS

❝If you're walking down the right path and you're willing to keep walking, eventually you'll make progress.❞

— *Barack Obama, March 18, 2008*

Many American presidents have come from humble beginnings. Everyone is taught the story of Abraham Lincoln in grade school and his log-cabin, rural upbringing. But perhaps no one's rise to the White House has been as amazing as that of Barrack Hussein Obama, who was born on August 4, 1961, to an American mother and Kenyan father in Hawaii. He not only became the first African American president but also the first to be born outside the continental United States.

His parents met while studying at the University of Hawaii. His father, also named Barack Hussein Obama, was studying as a foreign student on scholarship. The couple married but split up shortly after Obama was born.

Obama and his mother moved to Seattle, Washington, and his father moved back to Kenya after attending Harvard University. Only a few years later, Obama's mother—Ann Dunham—married an Indonesian man and they moved to Indonesia, with Obama, for several years. But Barack was shuttled back to Hawaii and was raised primarily by his grandparents as his mother continued her studies and field work as an anthropologist in Indonesia.

College Years

A good student, Obama—known as Barry to his friends—attended prestigious Columbia University in New York before going to law school at Harvard. Throughout

This undated photo shows Barack Obama (*right*) with his mother, half-sister, and stepfather in Indonesia.

his schooling, Obama took up several causes for the underprivileged and the disenfranchised and became very active in local politics, though not running for office. But it was here, living away from all his relatives, that he began to fight to find his own identity.

"Away from my mother, away from my grandparents, I was engaged in a fitful interior struggle. I was trying to raise myself to be a black man in America, and beyond the given of my appearance, no one around me seemed to know exactly what that meant," he wrote.[1]

Even though Obama spent more time with his grandparents than his birth parents, it was tough on the twenty-one-year-old Barack to lose his father to a car accident. Years later, he lost his mother to cancer.

Getting Involved in Politics

After graduating from Harvard with his law degree, Obama went to work in Chicago, Illinois, as the director of a developing communities program. There, he served as a community organizer, helping with tenant rights, job training, and college prep classes for high school students.

His work took him closer to the city's inner political circles. Even though he was still young, he decided to run for the Illinois State Senate in 1996; he was elected easily. There he went to work for the poor, gaining tax credits for childcare and working on reforming welfare and medical benefits for the people in his district.

He won re-election in 1998, but in 2000 he lost a bid for the US Congress. He ran successfully once again for the state senate in 2002, but in 2004 his wish to work on the national stage came true when he was elected

Kenya

Barack Obama's father was born in the African nation of Kenya. In 2015, during a visit to that country, President Obama exclaimed that he was the "first Kenyan-American president."

Kenya is an East African country that borders the Indian Ocean and five other countries including Tanzania, Uganda, South Sudan, Ethiopia, and Somalia. The population of Kenya is about 45 million people.

The country's climate is mainly hot, tropical, and humid as it sits very near the equator, though the grasslands are significantly cooler and snow exists on mountain tops. There is also a dry desert-like region near South Sudan.

European exploration resulted in the British Empire colonizing the region in the 1800s, and it became known as the Kenyan colony in the 1920s. Because of the British influence, English was the main language spoken for many years and remains one of two official languages.

After decades of British rule that saw white settlers control the power and economy of the country, unrest and rebellion started to emerge in the 1950s. Britain sent troops and weapons to the region to eventually squash the **rebellion,** but it was clear the country's citizens would not rest until they were given independence. That finally occurred in 1963 with Great Britain finally relinquishing its hold on the nation.

Continued on page 12

Continued from page 11

The country relies on its diverse and amazing wildlife to boost the economy; safaris and nature-themed vacations attract visitors from all over the world. Kenya is one of the few countries that is home to the "big five African game animals," consisting of elephants, leopards, lions, buffalo, and rhinoceros.

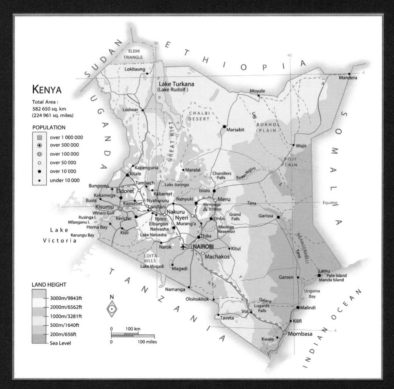

A map shows the African nation of Kenya, where Barack Obama's father was born.

to the US Senate. It was a stunning victory from a rela-tively unknown politician who won the seat in a landslide. Obama became only the fifth black US senator in history.[2]

It was 2004, nearly three years after the terrorist attacks of 9/11 thrust the United States into the forefront of the war on terrorism. The unity of the nation in the months after the attacks had dissipated, and the country was split on whether the strategy of a war in Afghanistan and one in Iraq was actually working.

Entering the National Stage

President George W. Bush was running for reelection and winning was no sure thing. The Democratic Party put up a strong candidate in Massachusetts senator John Kerry. But the person who stole the show at the 2004 Democratic National Convention was a junior senator from Illinois by the name of Barack Obama. He delivered the keynote address on the second night of the convention, and after the twenty-minute speech that detailed his vision for America, just about everyone knew his name.

His speech united the party and seemed to energize the country. His speech made it okay to oppose how the country was waging the war on terror. One of the highlights was this passage:

> "Well, I say to them tonight, there is not a liberal America and a conservative America—there is the United States of America. There is not a black America and a white America and Latino America and Asian America— there's the United States of America.

The pundits like to slice-and-dice our country into Red States and Blue States; Red States for Republicans, Blue States for Democrats. But I've got news for them, too: We worship an awesome God in the Blue States, and we don't like federal agents poking around in our libraries in the Red States. We coach Little League in the Blue States, and, yes, we've got some gay friends in the Red States. There are patriots who opposed the war in Iraq and there are patriots who supported the war in Iraq."[3]

Despite energy from Obama's words, Kerry was defeated by Bush in the November presidential election. Still, the speech and Obama's fresh, new attitude catapulted him to the forefront of the Democratic Party.

And as President Bush's war on terrorism—which included sending American troops to fight in Afghanistan and Iraq—grew more unpopular with the American public, it became clear that the country would soon be headed in a new direction.

Running for President

In 2007, Barack Obama announced his intention to run for the office of president of the United States. Among the major themes of his campaign was the war on terror, specifically his opposition to American troops fighting what seemed to be an endless war in Iraq. His main challenger within the party came from Hillary Clinton. The two candidate debated and disagreed on many issues, but Obama's campaign stressing hope and change won out, and Clinton dropped out of the race.

Hillary Clinton

US Senator and future 2016 presidential candidate Hillary Clinton speaks to an organization several months before the 9/11 attacks.

To reach the White House and become the first African American president of the United States, Barack Obama had to defeat politician and former first lady Hillary Clinton for the Democratic Party's nomination.

Clinton would again run for the presidency eight years later in the 2016 election. Her husband, William Jefferson Clinton, known as Bill, was the country's forty-second president. Her husband served in the White House from 1993 to 2001.

Continued on page 16

Continued from page 15

Hillary Diane Rodham was born on October 26, 1947, in Park Ridge, Illinois. She graduated from Wellesley College and earned a law degree from Yale University.

She married Bill Clinton and he became the governor of Arkansas. After eight years as the country's First Lady, Hillary Clinton was elected a US Senator from New York, where she relocated, having the distinction of being the first woman to serve in that capacity. She was re-elected four years later and served in that position for eight years.

In 2001, shortly after the terrorist attacks of September 11, she voted to authorize the war in Afghanistan that marked the beginning of the country's war on terrorism.

After losing the Democratic nomination to Obama in 2008, she agreed to serve as his secretary of state, one of the highest and most respected positions in the country's government.

Her reign as secretary of state and as a presidential candidate was not without controversy. She was investigated by the Federal Bureau of Investigation (FBI) for conducting government business using a private email server and for her handling of a crisis at an American embassy in Libya that was overrun and several Americans murdered.

In 2016 she ran for president once again, winning the party nomination, but she was defeated by Donald Trump.

Barack Obama waves to the crowd shortly after learning that he had successfully won the election for president of the United States.

The issue of the war on terrorism was a central theme throughout the campaign process. Obama's Republican opponent was Arizona senator John McCain, who was a war hero and a war prisoner during the Vietnam War.

Both men agreed that the war on terrorism was not being waged effectively, but both had different ideas on how to proceed. Obama was clear. He wanted fewer troops overseas fighting in Iraq and Afghanistan.

There was a lot of ugly rhetoric during the campaign, including accusations and rumors that Obama was not really American and that his middle name—Hussein—showed he had ties to the Arab world and possibly terrorism. McCain defended Obama and told crowds that he was not an Arab, yet the rumors and the stigma stuck for years. This was, in some ways, because of Obama's strategy on how he wanted to wage the war on terror—one his opponents said he was losing.

That November, Obama defeated McCain and became the first African American to be elected president of the United States.

A WAR INHERITED

> **"I have always believed that hope is that stubborn thing inside us that insists, despite all the evidence to the contrary, that something better awaits us so long as we have the courage to keep reaching, to keep working, to keep fighting."**
>
> —*Barack Obama, victory speech, November 7, 2012*

So, what did Barack Obama inherit when he took over the presidency in January 2009? The country's health care system was in need of reform. The economy was in shambles and in the midst of a recession caused in part by bad loans granted by overzealous banking corporations. But the issue that was at the forefront of many Americans' minds was terrorism.

How would this new president keep Americans safe? How would Barack Obama defeat the terrorists? Would

Al-Qaeda and Taliban prisoners have been kept by American forces at a naval base in Guantanamo, Cuba, since the war on terror began.

the mastermind of the 9/11 attacks, Osama bin Laden, ever be brought to justice?

While the vast majority of Americans resumed their daily activities in the weeks and months following the 9/11 attacks, there was still an underlying tension and fear that terrorists could strike again without warning.

But there were other issues as well. President Obama had pledged to close down the US makeshift military prison in Guantanamo Bay, Cuba.

Guantanamo Bay

Shortly after the 9/11 attacks, President Bush needed a place to detain prisoners captured during the war on terrorism. Some were Taliban fighters, others were part of Osama bin Laden's network of terror—a group known as al-Qaeda.

The Bush administration decided that the US Naval base on the southern tip of Cuba, a place called Guantanamo Bay, would serve as a military prison. Why Cuba? Well, by not detaining these prisoners in the United States, the government could keep them indefinitely without a trial and perhaps even use interrogation tactics that would not be legal in the United States. In fact, by the end of 2016, some of those prisoners believed to have been involved in the planning of the 9/11 attacks were still being held at the base without ever having gone to trial.[1]

Almost immediately, the prison came under fire by critics and human rights advocates. They said the United States was not following the code of the Geneva Convention. When Obama was elected president, he vowed to shut the prison down. But eight years later it was still operating as a prison, mainly because of opposition from Congress to closing it down.[2]

In addition to dealing with Guantanamo Bay, the new president took over his job while the United States was involved in two costly and bloody ground wars—in Iraq and Afghanistan. Also, the leader of the attacks on 9/11, Osama bin Laden, was still free, releasing taunting propaganda videos every so often.

Geneva Convention

You may have heard the term "Geneva Convention," in the news, your history books, or even old war movies. So, what exactly does it mean?

Geneva is a large city in the country of Switzerland that sits in the shadow of the Swiss Alps. The city has come to be known as the center for diplomacy. It is the headquarters for several organizations including the European United Nations and the Red Cross.

The Geneva Conventions are basically a series of treaties and agreements that protect the rights of individuals during wartime. They are international guidelines calling for countries to treat people humanely. In all, they consist of four treaties, but most of us refer to the 1949 agreement simply as the Geneva Convention.

This agreement, agreed to wholly or in part by nearly 200 countries, said that prisoners of war—whether they be soldiers or civilians—have the right to be treated humanely. It also protects the rights of civilians living near war zones and provides rules for how countries should treat wounded soldiers of their enemies.

The reason this agreement was needed was a direct result of the wartime atrocities committed by Germany and Japan during World War II. The Nazi regime in Germany shocked the world by building

Continued on page 23

Continued from page 22

death camps where they exterminated millions of Jews during the Holocaust. They also used the Jews to perform slave labor.

The Japanese were accused of targeting officers and medics during battles as well as torturing prisoners taken during battle.

The detaining of terror prisoners at the military prison in Guantanamo Bay has come under fire by those who say it violates the Geneva Convention. The United States responded by arguing that the terrorists are not protected because they do not represent a specific country, do not wear military uniforms, and target innocent people to kill.[3]

Filling the Cabinet

One of the first things any new president does is fill out his cabinet. The cabinet are the advisers the president appoints to very important positions, such as the secretary of the treasury, the secretary of education, and so on. Arguably the two most important cabinet positions—especially when fighting a war, are the secretary of state and the secretary of defense.

Obama appointed his one-time rival Hillary Clinton to the post of secretary of state, meaning she would represent the United States in many foreign matters as the country's top diplomat.

But, in a historic move, Obama decided to retain Bush's secretary of defense Robert Gates. It was the first time an opposing party had ever kept a defense secretary in the same position.

But Obama's thinking was simple. This was a crucial time in American history, and that particular position needed some continuity.[4] And actually, it represented a continuation of the good will that President Bush wanted to impart on the new president.

Still, it's interesting to note that Gates actually turned in his letter of resignation before continuing the position under the Obama administration but the president rejected it and asked him to remain in his position. One of the main reasons Gates was leery of continuing at his post was that the Bush and Obama presidencies had such different ideology.[5]

After all, the Bush administration was in favor of escalation and sending more troops, if deemed necessary, to the war zones. President Obama, on the other hand, wanted to fight the war on terrorism in a different manner and was planning a massive reduction in the number of soldiers fighting on foreign soil.

Military and defense expert Michael O'Hanlon said keeping Gates in the same position was a great idea.

"It suggests an awareness of the importance of continuity at a time of war, plus a healthy respect for Gates," he said.[6]

For some reason, perhaps due to the inherent impatience of people, there is a lot of emphasis placed on what new presidents can accomplish during their first 100 days in office. This is despite the fact that presidents are elected

Transition from Bush to Obama

After President George W. Bush's second term, the Republican Party was set to pass the torch of leadership to President-elect Barack Obama and the Democratic Party.

This is not always a pleasant or amiable time as the different parties are not always eager to ease the transition of the next governing party into power. But with the war on terror continuing to be waged in several areas by American forces, cooperation transcended party politics.

But, by all accounts, the transition between the Bush and Obama presidencies may have been one of the smoothest of all time. Apparently, Bush went out of his way to assist Obama, helping the new administration receive security clearances and hosting the president-elect and his wife, Michelle, at the White House for special meetings and tours.

One of the two main reasons for the unprecedented cooperation between the Bush and Obama administrations can be tied directly to the war on terrorism.

The 9/11 Commission recommended legislation that was passed into law by Congress that required enhanced cooperation to ensure the country's safety against future potential terrorist attacks.

The second? Well, Bush experienced virtually no cooperation from the Clinton administration and experts have speculated that lack of cooperation hurt Bush's ability to govern the country during his first 100 days in office.

Continued on page 26

Continued from page 25

President George W. Bush shows newly elected President Barack Obama around the White House during what would be a seamless transition period.

to four-year terms and that oftentimes accomplishments cannot be judged until many years later. Still, Obama was no different and wanted to show the American people that they had made the correct choice. His plan for fighting the war on terrorism would be different. He wanted to end the interrogation tactics used on prisoners and he wanted to close the prison at Guantanamo Bay.

So, on his third day in office, on January 22, 2009, the new president signed an executive order to close down Guantanamo Bay within one year. He said prisons like that one, as well as torture-like techniques to make prisoners give up crucial information, made Americans no better than terrorists.[7]

"We are not ... going to continue with a false choice between our safety and our ideals," he said while signing the order. "We think that it is precisely our ideals that give us the strength and the moral high ground to be able to effectively deal with the unthinking violence that we see emanating from terrorist organizations around the world."[8]

Still Obama was faced with the tough choice with what to do about the two wars American troops were fighting in Iraq and Afghanistan. He had promised to bring back all US soldiers from Iraq. Realistically, thought, the country was still very unstable, and a chaotic civil war would destabilize the region further and potentially become even more of a hot spot for terrorism.

To make matters worse, American soldiers were not faring very well in Afghanistan. The Taliban and al-Qaeda seemed to be gaining strength, and supposed US allies in the region—like Pakistan—were providing little or no help in crushing the terrorists.

Obama had repeatedly said those two wars and the overall war on terrorism were conflicts the United States could not afford to lose. He said that military actions had to be coupled with diplomacy in order to be effective. But the previous president had sent billions of dollars of aid and incentives to the impoverished nation of Pakistan, with little result. President Obama needed a new plan and he wanted it in action during his first 100 days.

With little military experience, Obama called a meeting of his top military leaders and national security personnel. He asked them a simple question: "What is the end game?"[9]

In other words, Obama wanted advice on winning the war on terrorism once and for all.

SHIFTING THE FOCUS

> **"Change will not come if we wait for some other person, or if we wait for some other time. We are the ones we've been waiting for. We are the change that we seek."**
>
> *— Barack Obama, 2008 campaign trail*

Almost immediately, the president came to the realization that he would not be able to fulfill his campaign promise of bringing all American soldiers home from Iraq. The fighting was still fierce at times and the country remained too unstable.

One of the difficulties in trying to keep the peace in Iraq after American forces toppled the government of dictator Saddam Hussein were the vast number of religious groups and sects that did not care for one another. These factions had already started claiming land or trying to settle old scores with the government in transition.

This map highlights the Taliban stronghold of Afghanistan. Afghanistan is bordered by Iran, Pakistan, Tajikistan, Uzbekistan, Turkmenistan, and China.

There was no real way to pull out of Iraq in 2009 or even 2010 for that matter. Many American military men and women would have to remain there, fighting insurgents and pockets of resistance. Also, the president would now have to send many from one hot spot to another by shifting resources to Afghanistan, the apparent headquarters for the forces of terror the United States was at war with.

Afghanistan

The war on terror may have spread to numerous countries around the globe and against several government and non-government-sponsored organizations, but it got its start in the stark, mountainous nation of Afghanistan.

Afghanistan is a central-Asian landlocked nation with a population of roughly thirty-two million people that is bordered by Pakistan, Iran, Turkmenistan, Uzbekistan, Tajikistan, and China.

Humans have inhabited the area known as Afghanistan since the Middle Paleolithic Era, also known as the Middle Stone Age, which spans the period that began about 300,000 years ago to 30,000 years ago.

In addition to being one of the earliest places where humanity existed, the country, with its strategic location, has also put it at the center of numerous military expeditions. Some of the leaders of countries that have waged war in this region include Alexander the Great, Mauryas, Genghis Khan and his Mongol army, the British Empire, the Soviet Union, and most recently the US-led anti-terrorism coalitions.

There have been attempts throughout history to modernize Afghanistan and attempts to bring the country on par with some of the area's other powers, but they have all failed. The country today

Continued on page 32

Continued from page 31

remains mired in poverty, disarray, and civil strife and war.

In the year 642, Arabs brought the religion of Islam to the region, replacing Buddhism as the primary belief system, and it has been prominent ever since. By the eleventh century, the region was known as one of the great centers of the Islamic world, but there were never really any great periods of peace. There are so many different tribal areas and different factions of Islam that caused—and continue to cause—constant conflict.

Afghanistan and Pakistan

So, after meeting with his military advisers, President Obama decided to send an additional 21,000 soldiers and marines to Afghanistan. He also deployed American non-military workers to the war-torn country to help rebuild and stabilize the government. Having a strong leadership and a thriving economy would be one way to ensure that terrorists could no longer use Afghanistan as a base.[1]

Obama also decided to continue the strategy of sending money and other forms of aid to neighboring Pakistan. This was despite the fact that American leaders could not fully trust the Pakistani government to cooperate in the war on terrorism. There was evidence that many Taliban and al-Qaeda forces had sought refuge just within Pakistan's borders and that Pakistan's government was not only turning a blind eye but offering them assistance and safe passage.

While this frustrated American leaders, they also knew that alienating Pakistan would only help to create yet another unstable country in the region where terrorism could take root and flourish.

Secretary Hillary Clinton even went as far as to call Pakistan a "mortal threat to the United States." Still, Obama pledged billions of dollars to the struggling country.[2]

Despite not accomplishing exactly what he had promised—troops were still fighting in Iraq—the new president was praised by many in the press for being flexible and willing to adjust his policies and strategies.

American soldiers patrol an area during the early days of the Iraq War.

Despite the good grades and smooth transition, it was still evident that the terror threat from al-Qaeda was not going away. In fact, the terror group was expanding throughout Asia and into Africa. And one of the really frustrating things about it was that they were using American weapons against the very country that once supplied them with the tools of war.

Almost immediately, President Obama's investment in the Pakistani government and military paid off. That February, Pakistani forces came away with a decisive and extremely one-sided victory against Taliban and al-Qaeda terrorists who had created a stronghold in the Pakistani city of Bajaur. Terrorists had taken over the city and it was their largest headquarters outside of Afghanistan.

And although the battle started before Obama took office, it was perhaps his investment that inspired the Pakistani troops to wipe out the enemy in that region. It was a crippling blow to the terrorists. In all, the terrorists lost 1,500 fighters while the Pakistani military lost only 97. That's about as lopsided as a battle can get.

A Change in Strategy

Just a few months later, however, in a curious shift in policy, the Obama administration stopped using the term "war on terrorism." They instead insisted they were at war with al-Qaeda. Obama's strategy involved distancing himself from President George W. Bush's policies and rhetoric. Instead Obama focused on keeping his promises to the American people that American forces would soon be coming home.[3]

Al-Qaeda

The United States supplied Osama bin Laden with weapons and financing while he was leading resistance fighters in combat against the former Soviet Union, which had invaded the country in 1979. It was a bloody and costly war that saw the mighty Soviet army defeated and sent back home after ten years.

But, instead of gaining an ally in bin Laden, the United States armed a future enemy. In 1988, bin Laden formed al-Qaeda, a Muslim group of fighters whose goal was to create one united Islamic state that would eventually go to war with the Western nations, such as Europe and the United States.[4]

Continued on page 36

Terrorist mastermind Osama bin Laden is shown on television praising the 9/11 attacks on Americans.

Continued from page 35

The group wanted to rid all Western influences from the Arab and Muslim world. They wanted their women to be covered up, they shunned Western-style clothing, and they were not bashful about laying out their bloody and violent goals.

In 1998, the World Islamic Front group issued a statement under the name "Jihad Against the Jews and Crusaders" that said it was the absolute duty of all Muslims to kill US citizens, even civilians, everywhere.[5]

Starting around that time, the group began to carry out deadly attacks, mainly against American targets. They planted bombs at US embassies in several countries, including Kenya. They bombed an American naval vessel docked in Yemen. The attacks killed hundreds.

But that would pale in both scope and number of victims in the years that followed. As documented earlier, the terror group was responsible for the 9/11 attacks that toppled the World Trade Center, killing thousands.

But they also were responsible for deadly bus bombs planted in the United Kingdom and attacks elsewhere. Their numbers grew in countries around the world.

The group remained active even after bin Laden's death, though many members later joined ISIS, or the Islamic State terror group.

Instead of the Bush strategy of using sheer force and numbers to overwhelm the enemy as well as questionable interrogation methods, President Obama decided he would be doing things differently.

Instead of a war, it was as if he instructed his military experts to devise counterterrorism policies. He would go after terrorist leaders and their money, and use intelligence to gather information. He would work the diplomatic front and forge alliances where there were none before. He wanted the American people to trust his war and not be afraid their privacies were being invaded.[6]

With the war in Afghanistan ramping up and things in Iraq settling down, the president decided it was soon time to come through on one of his campaign promises. He announced that American troops would soon be leaving Iraq. Most Americans believed the war in Iraq—initiated by Bush—was a colossal mistake. There were never any weapons of mass destruction found and while toppling the tyrannical dictator Saddam Hussein was seen as an overall good, the war took American resources away from battling the true enemies: the Taliban and al-Qaeda.

Some even blamed the war in Iraq for making al-Qaeda stronger and more of a global force. And while most also agreed that American soldiers needed to come home from the war in Iraq, there were those who believed it would be a mistake to prematurely leave the country without a stable government and economy in place.

That was the main criticism of US Sen. John McCain, who ran unsuccessfully against Obama for the presidency. McCain, a former military man with a lot of war experience, said over and over that it would be a mistake to announce exactly when soldiers would be leaving Iraq or any other conflict or war zone for that matter. He said the enemy forces would simply wait out American troops and lay low until the American presence was gone. He would later say that wars do not end because politicians say so.[7]

He wasn't the only one to disagree with Obama's announcement that American troops would be gone from Iraq by the end of 2011.

"(The) announcement that we will remove all of our forces from Iraq is a political decision and not a military one," said Minnesota congresswoman Michele Bachmann in a statement at the time. "It represents the complete failure of President Obama to secure an agreement with Iraq for our troops to remain there to preserve the peace and demonstrates how far our foreign policy leadership has fallen."[8]

The American public was indeed tired of war and leery of seeing reports of American military personnel killed in action. But would the president's insistence on bringing home American troops in a timely manner make the world safer in the long term? That would be debated in the years to come.

MANHUNT

> **Evil does exist in the world. A non-violent movement could not have halted Hitler's armies. Negotiations cannot convince al-Quaeda's leaders to lay down their arms.**

With American forces bogged down in Afghanistan and the American public tired of hearing and reading about this war without an end in sight, patience was running thin. Not only were Americans still being killed in far off battles, but the man that just about everyone held responsible for it all—Osama bin Laden—was still alive and free to conduct al-Qaeda attacks around the globe. In addition, bin Laden would taunt the United States every so often with a video message promising more murder and mayhem inflicted on Americans.

The Bush administration had tried for nearly eight years to track him down and bring him to justice, but they failed. The Obama administration made similar promises to capture the world's most wanted man.

The Americans nearly captured him a few months after the 9/11 terror attacks that killed thousands. It was in Afghanistan, during the Battle of Tora Bora. Somehow he managed to elude the Americans and escaped. He went into hiding soon after, once he felt the intensity of the manhunt. It is believed he moved often from one al-Qaeda safe house to another during the next ten years, mainly in Afghanistan and Pakistan.

Who Was Osama bin Laden?

But who was Osama bin Laden? The son of a Saudi billionaire and reported to have close to fifty brothers and sisters, bin Laden left his privileged life to help Muslims in Afghanistan fight off Soviet invaders in the 1980s. Backed by American support, bin Laden became empowered by the victory over the Soviets and thought it was a sign that the Muslim world would rise to power.[1]

That was when he turned his attention to toppling the United States as the world's leading superpower. Protected by the hardline religious zealots in Afghanistan known as the Taliban, bin Laden formed al-Qaeda in Afghanistan.

Before this, terrorism had always been state-sponsored, or backed up and supported by a particular government. Osama bin Laden did the exact opposite. It was as if his terror group supported Afghanistan.[2]

By the mid-1990s, according to American law enforcement agencies, bin Laden was considered the most dangerous terrorist in the world. He also was believed to have been behind a foiled plot to kill President Bill Clinton and a failed attempt to blow up the World Trade Center.[3]

Osama bin Laden is believed to have been behind a failed plot to kill President Bill Clinton.

In 1998, bin Laden declared that it was the right and duty of every Muslim to kill Americans and their allies whether they were civilians or military.[4] By masterminding and ordering the attacks that toppled the World Trade Center on 9/11, bin Laden and his minions believed it would force the United States to give up its interests in the mainly Muslim Middle East and remove all of its armed forces.

And while the terror of September 11, 2001, was clearly bin Laden's greatest victory, there are some who say it was also his biggest downfall. Instead of retreating and giving in to his terror, the American people were resolved more than ever to eliminate terrorism and bring bin Laden's reign to an end. President Bush vowed that bin Laden would one day be brought to justice.

His followers were helpless. They were forced to swear allegiance to him just as many Nazis were made to swear allegiance to Adolph Hitler. In fact, they also referred to him as "prince" and would seek his permission before speaking. In a way, they were prisoner to his every whim.

His attacks may have actually brought about the end to al-Qaeda.[5]

Three Choices

After years spent on intelligence gathering, missed opportunities, and failed attempts to kill or capture bin Laden, the Central Intelligence Agency, or the CIA, believed they knew where the world's most wanted terrorist might be hiding. They passed on the information to President Obama three days before the fateful raid that would rid the world of bin Laden once and for all.

The president's most trusted advisers gave him three options to deal with the information. The first option was to continue watching the compound in a wealthy Pakistan neighborhood where they believed he might be staying. The second option was to target the compound and bomb it from planes. The third option was to send in a team of Navy Seals on a clandestine mission to take him out.

All three options had their level of risk and reward, and Obama agonized over the decision for the next few days. Watching the compound seemed like the most prudent

The Taliban

This group of fundamental Islamic hardliners emerged as an organized force in northern Pakistan along the Afghan border shortly after the Soviet armed forces left Afghanistan in the early 1990s.

The group is in favor of restoring Sharia, or Islamic, law. They were originally made up of the Pashtun people, a large ethnic group or tribe that has existed for a very long time in southern Afghanistan. The movement to return to such strict, unforgiving religious rules is believed to have started in religious schools in Saudi Arabia. Wealthy Saudis are supposed to have funded the movement, as it falls in line with the belifes of the majority of Sunni Muslims.[6]

Other Muslim groups include mainly Sunnis, Shiites, and Sufis. Oftentimes the groups do not get along, and they have resorted to violence to settle differences.

The Taliban rule by fear and intimidation in addition to faith. The men are required to grow long beards and women have to cover every inch of their bodies—except for their eyes—by wearing burkas.

Television, music, and movies are not allowed, and those found guilty of crimes are punished publicly and severely, including public executions. Those caught stealing typically lose a hand or an arm.[7]

Once girls reach the age of ten, they are no longer permitted to attend school. The power and influence of the Taliban has gone up and down since the 2001 terror attacks on the United States carried out by al-Qaeda.

One of the more publicized atrocities of the Taliban was shooting Pakistani schoolgirl Malala Yousafzai in the face for continuing to go to school. She survived and is now a symbol for women's rights against Islamic law.

President Barack Obama applauds during an annual White House Correspondent's Dinner in 2011.

approach, though the risk was that the information would be leaked and bin Laden would escape before American forces could verify his presence.

The second option of bombing the home would carry the risk of civilian casualties, accidentally killing Pakistani citizens living near the compound. There was also the risk that the occupants would not be able to be identified.

No, President Obama wanted to be sure. Even though the third option seemed the riskiest and American lives could be lost, he opted to send in the Navy Seals in the dead of night to kill or capture the world's most wanted man. This was especially tricky, and could have proven politically calamitous, as the assault would be done in a sovereign country—a supposed ally—without their knowledge. But the mission was too sensitive and there was no way the United States could risk being betrayed by someone in the Pakistani government. The mission would be called Operation Neptune Spear in honor of the Navy Seals, and bin Laden would be referred to as "Geronimo" if he was killed or captured.

The Special Forces unit had already been practicing the assault on a replica of the compound in which they believed bin Laden to be hiding. So, during the early morning hours, four American helicopters—specially modified to be virtually silent—took off from a base in Afghanistan and cut through the cloudy night on their way to catch bin Laden.[8]

President Obama had to keep the mission a secret from almost everyone. He couldn't risk someone accidentally spilling the beans on social media and alerting the enemy. In fact, as the raid was getting started, Obama made his annual appearance at a special White House dinner for the media. He looked calm and cool and even cracked a few jokes.

But, as soon as he was able, the president was whisked to the Situation Room where he watched on silent screens as the night's events unfolded before him and his most trusted advisers.

The mission started out in nightmarish fashion when one of the helicopters malfunctioned as it was landing within the compound's walls and crashed. No one was injured, but the chopper was disabled. The president watched silently as the Seals blew holes into the sides of the buildings and ventured inside.

President Barack Obama watches live footage as American forces close in on terrorist Osama bin Laden, who is killed that very night.

The Situation Room

Even before Osama bin Laden was killed by American forces, we'd all seen versions of "The Situation Room" in movies and television shows. It always depicts the American president having to make tough decisions regarding dangerous operations or unfolding situations. Sometimes it is seen as a deep underground bunker. Sometimes it is shown as a small space, cramped with the president and his closest advisers.

In reality, it is a 5,000-square-foot room in the West Wing of the White House, also known as the John F. Kennedy Conference Room. It is the room where the president and his or her top advisers monitor crisis events around the world that normally involve American interests.

The room is equipped with state-of-the-art technology and communications equipment that allow the president the ability to communicate with and command—if necessary—American military forces around the world.

The room was created by President John F. Kennedy in 1961 after a botched invasion of Cuba. The disastrous Bay of Pigs invasion was blamed on the lack of information made available to the president as the invasion was taking place. The room is monitored twenty-four hours a day by "watch teams" who keep an eye on domestic and international events and keep the president and his staff updated at all times.

While the actions taken in the Situation Room are oftentimes remarkable, the daily activities are usually routine. Each day begins the same way. The president is given a daily book every morning with updates and intelligence from around the globe.

The grainy, unstable images that were being transmitted back to the Situation Room lit up with gunfire and apparent chaos. President Obama and his advisors had no idea what was going on. Then, much to the relief of everyone, a voice came through with a transmission, saying "visual on Geronimo."[9]

Osama bin Laden had been shot and killed. A relieved President Obama now wanted to share the news with the American people as soon as he could.

KILLING BIN LADEN

"The death of bin Laden marks the most significant achievement to date in our nation's effort to defeat al-Qaeda."

—*Barack Obama, announcing the death of bin Laden, May 2, 2011*

It was nearly midnight on May 2, 2011, but that didn't matter to President Obama. He knew the American people would want to hear the news that a manhunt that lasted more than ten years was finally over.

The terrorist who plotted and successfully carried out the 9/11 attacks, which killed thousands, was finally dead. By no means did anyone believe it would be the end of the war on terrorism, but it was still a milestone victory, one that should be recognized and even celebrated according to many.

Never had there been such a manhunt and such an effort to catch one man and bring him to justice. It's hard to remember anyone in present history who was so reviled in the United States as Osama bin Laden.

Late-Night Announcement

"Good evening," a somber-looking President Obama began. "Tonight, I can report to the American people and to the world that the United States has conducted an operation that killed Osama bin Laden, the leader of al-Qaeda and a terrorist who's responsible for the murder of thousands of innocent men, women, and children."[1]

Obama took great care to remember those families who suffered the most at the hands of bin Laden and his network of terror. He would later say that he hoped bin Laden thought of the 9/11 terror victims in the moments before he was shot and killed. He continued his address:

"The American people did not choose this fight. It came to our shores, and started with the senseless slaughter of our citizens. After nearly ten years of service, struggle, and sacrifice, we know well the costs of war. These efforts weigh on me every time I, as Commander-in-Chief, have to sign a letter to a family that has lost a loved one, or look into the eyes of a service member who's been gravely wounded.

So Americans understand the costs of war. Yet as a country, we will never tolerate our security being threatened, nor stand idly by when our people have been killed. We will be relentless in defense of our citizens and our friends and allies. We will be true to the values that make us who we are. And on nights like this one, we can say to those families who

Celebrations, like this one in New York, took place around the United States after the news was broadcast that Osama bin Laden had been killed.

have lost loved ones to al-Qaeda's terror: Justice has been done."[2]

Bin Laden's body was taken by American forces and buried at sea. The reasoning was they did not want his burial site to become some sort of shrine where extremists and militants could gather for generations to come and draw inspiration for violent acts.

The news of bin Laden's death traveled quickly, and spontaneous celebrations erupted all over the United States, despite the late hour. In New York alone, celebrations popped up at Times Square and at Ground Zero—the site of the former World Trade Center. People hugged, sang the national anthem and chanted U-S-A, U-S-A in scenes reminiscent of the victorious end of World War II.

Others burned pictures of bin Laden and passersby honked horns and cheered wildly. Even boats churning up and down the Hudson River blew their horns in celebration.[3]

Critics in the United States and around the world questioned whether someone's death should be cheered as bin Laden's was. But for the American people, it was a long-awaited moment of triumph. There had been so much hatred and so much effort for ten years to catch bin laden that there were many who thought they would never live to see the day.

In his speech, President Obama did warn that the war on terrorism was far from over.

"For over two decades, bin Laden has been al-Qaeda's leader and symbol, and has continued to plot attacks against our country and our friends and allies. The death of bin Laden marks the most significant achievement to date in our nation's effort to defeat al-Qaeda.

Yet his death does not mark the end of our effort. There's no doubt that al-Qaeda will continue to pursue attacks against us. We must—and we will—remain vigilant at home and abroad."[4]

His words would prove prophetic. But for now the mood would be celebratory. Over the next few weeks there was a lot of attention and rightful praise placed on the Special Forces Unit that carried out the attack: Seal Team Six.

What was interesting to many about bin Laden's death was how he was actually living. Despite being videotaped continuously amid rugged mountainous backdrops and preaching that his followers embrace the suffering and hardships that would eventually lead to victory, he was

Seal Team Six

The term Seal Team Six for the elite naval fighting force has become synonymous with heroism. The fighters, known for their bravery, will always be remembered as the team that brought down and killed Osama bin Laden.

They are the US Navy's equivalent to the army's Delta Force. The group's official name is the United States Naval Special Warfare Development Group The name "Seal Team Six" was disbanded in the 1990s, but that's still what everyone calls the special

Continued on page 54

Special forces with Seal Team Six see some action. This is the elite unit that killed Osama bin Laden.

Continued from page 53

fighting force. The force was formed in 1980 after the end of the Iranian hostage crisis.

Once known as a small group that was good for highly specialized missions, Seal Team Six—a classified special operations force—has become known as one of the most clandestine spy groups as well as the best man hunters in the world.[5]

The group is comprised of about 300 assault troops and 1,500 support personnel.[6]

Over the last decade or two, the group has really ramped up its activity, including very dangerous undercover and spy missions. They are so good at what they do that the group's members have been referred to as invisible warriors.

They move about in a variety of non-obvious ways, including in commercial fishing boats, as husband and wife, and as employees for companies.[7]

In the years after the bin Laden assassination, the group has come under fire for some of their methods, including not taking better care to ensure the safety of civilians during their operations.

living in a million-dollar estate with satellite television, DVDs, and access to all types of movies, many of which are forbidden under Taliban rule.

He was also staying just a few miles from the Pakistan intelligence headquarters and was neighbors with many high-ranking officers in Pakistan's armed forces. There were real questions among Obama and his advisers about whether the Pakistani government was hiding bin Laden or at least knew that he was staying there.

What Did bin Laden's Death Mean?

In any event, while al-Qaeda lost its charismatic leader and founder, bin Laden's death spawned two important revelations regarding the war on terrorism. The first was that the world, and especially the enemies of the United States, were put on notice that the United States was resolved to hunt down its enemies regardless of how many years it took. The second offshoot, unfortunately, was that bin Laden's death splintered the terror network, causing numerous violent extremist groups to take up the cause of destroying the Western world.

"Five years after the killing of Osama bin Laden, it's not wrong to be fairly pessimistic in our outlook on the world," said Matthew Henman, head of a group that analyzes international security risks.

Added James Clapper, the director of National Intelligence, in addressing US Senators: "There are now more Sunni violent extremist groups, members, and safe havens than at any time in history."[8]

One of those groups would come to be known as ISIS (also known as ISIL), a terror organization determined to take American lives.

In a way, killing bin Laden failed to produce the effect and ultimate result the United States was after, much like bin Laden failed to achieve his ultimate goals when he ordered terrorists to fly planes into the Twin Towers, toppling them forever.

Leon Panetta

During President Obama's speech to the American people announcing the death of Osama bin Laden, he mentioned the name Leon Panetta as being a key cog in the hunt for bin Laden.

But just who was Leon Panetta? And why was the president thanking him?

Panetta had long been a familiar name and face in Washington politics. He was a lawyer, adviser, and former member of Congress for fifteen years. But when Obama nominated the experienced

President Obama praised CIA head Leon Panetta for his work in finding and killing Osama bin Laden.

Continued from page 56

statesman to head the Central Intelligence Agency (CIA), there were more than a few raised eyebrows. Even Panetta himself questioned why the president would choose someone with such little intelligence experience to lead the CIA, especially during a war.[10]

Despite that lack of experience, it was under Panetta's watch and leadership that the CIA was able to gather enough information about the whereabouts of bin Laden to launch Operation Neptune Spear.

It was also during Panetta's tenure that—under his recommendation—the United States increased its use of drones to bomb targets along the border of Pakistan and Afghanistan.

As the head of a secretive agency charged with gathering intelligence and keeping the country safe from further terror attacks, Panetta disagreed publicly with some of the harsh interrogation methods used under the Bush administration. However, in a memoir written years after he left office, Panetta did admit that the tactics yielded very useful information about al-Qaeda and their network of terror.

Panetta was later named as Obama's secretary of defense, but upon retiring he wrote a memoir extremely critical of Obama and how he handled the war on terrorism.[11]

More and more countries in the Middle East and Asia became destabilized over the next few years, providing fertile grounds for terror groups to recruit from.

Obama was often criticized for leaning too heavily on the bin Laden success and not being harsh enough or quick enough to act with force against the other groups that have emerged. Apparently these criticisms bothered the president, and when confronted with questions about his commitment to fight terror, he would often respond: "ask Osama bin Laden."[9]

But the truth was that something would happen later that year, over the protestations of many of his advisers, that would prove to be a costly misstep in the war on terrorism.

CHAPTER
SIX

THE RISE OF ISIS

> **"Let's make two things clear. ISIL is not 'islamic.' No religion condones the killing of innocents, and the vast majority of ISIL's victims have been Muslim. And ISIL is certainly not a state."**
>
> *— Barack Obamaon on the anniversary of the 9/11 attacks, September 11, 2014*

While critics of the war on terrorism blame President George W. Bush's invasion of Iraq as causing the spread of al-Qaeda, the same critics blame the rise of ISIS on President Obama's decision to withdraw troops from the very same country.

ISIS, or the terror group known as the Islamic State, would not really rise until several years after President Obama's decision to withdraw all troops from Iraq in 2011. But, before, during and after his decision to withdraw, there was controversy.

Exactly when should US troops leave Iraq?

Was Iraq Ready?

It's true that the president wanted to honor his campaign pledge of bringing American troops home, but was Iraq ready for self-rule? Could their leaders police their own country and keep its own citizens—as well as the rest of the world—safe from extremism?

Still, when Obama was campaigning in 2008, the then-US senator vowed to be the one to end the war in Iraq. So, in 2010, after Iraq held its first free elections, the president decided it was time to take a hands-off approach

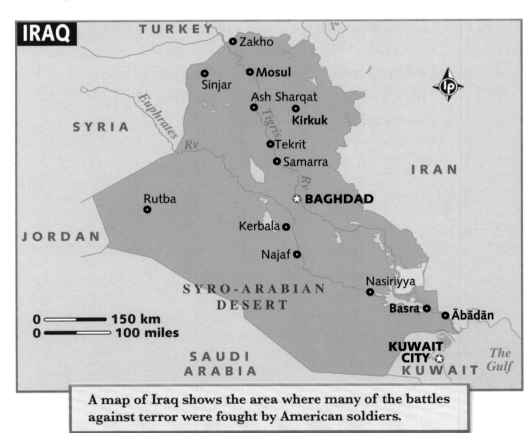

A map of Iraq shows the area where many of the battles against terror were fought by American soldiers.

to Iraqi politics. This was even as his critics argued that the country was not ready or stable enough.

But in addition to declaring that the military would be leaving, many American contractors and security and communications businesses decided to pull out as well. The result? There was a lack of international and American partnerships to really grow the economy.

Obama and his administration were warned that Iraq's prime minister, Nouri al-Maliki, was exhibiting power-hungry tendencies and his behavior might not be the stable force that Iraq needed. Deals to keep the peace between the Sunnis, Shiites, and Kurds were already very fragile.[1]

Some of America's allies in the region, like Kuwait and Saudi Arabia, were worried that a weakening Iraqi government might embolden Iran—Iraq's longtime enemy—to further destabilize the government.

Regardless of all the moving pieces, the American people were tired of this never-ending war on terrorism and applauded the president's words on October 21, 2011, when he announced American troops would be leaving Iraq for good.

"The United States is moving forward, from a position of strength," the president said. "The long war in Iraq will come to an end by the end of this year. The transition in Afghanistan is moving forward, and our troops are finally coming home. As they do, fewer deployments and more time training will help keep our military the very best in the world. And as we welcome home our newest veterans, we'll never stop working to give them and their families the care, the benefits, and the opportunities that they have earned."[2]

The announcement said the troops would be home by the end of the year.

At the time of his announcement, more than 4,400 US troops had been killed in action and the war cost American taxpayers $700 billion. No one knew for sure whether the sacrifice had been worth it. No one knew whether Iraq would falter or flourish.

By contrast, nearly 20,000 American soldiers lost their lives in World War II's the Battle of the Bulge, according to numerous historic sources.

When asked if the cost to American lives and money was worth it, one of the president's advisers, Anthony Blinken said: "History is going to have to judge."[3]

Prime Minister al-Maliki wanted Americans to leave as well. He refused to grant immunity from prosecution for any military "advisers" that Obama might have been tempted to leave behind to continue training Iraqi forces.

Unfortunately, old tensions and centuries-old conflicts did not go away as the last American soldiers left Iraq. And al-Maliki, a Shiite Muslim, started enacting policies that were favorable to Shiites and decidedly anti-Sunni. This was not a good way to start self-rule. He would eventually even accuse and charge some of his own advisers—Sunni Muslims—with offenses and have them arrested. Almost immediately, some of the leaders and top newspapers in the Arab world called on al-Maliki to resign.

Dr. Hichem Karoui, a leading expert and respected source when it comes to Middle East politics, said al-Maliki was "unfit" to rule, saying he treated Sunnis as "second-class citizens."

A US soldier stands guard against possible Taliban attackers during a ceremony.

"Iraq is still waiting for a real democratic government able to perform the task of giving the real figures of the population," he said. "This may hardly be the current government."[4]

A Long History

It's impossible to judge and grade President Obama's policies in the Middle East as part of the war on terrorism without really understanding the dynamic of the region and the precarious relationship with the United States.

There is no way to attempt to explain and analyze the relationship here but to say the history is long and often contentious. The United States' special relationship with

Iraq

The country of Iraq was never really a country until after World War I. And that is one of the reasons why the nation has long-been wracked with violence. The area that used to be part of the Ottoman Empire was occupied by British troops during World War I.

After the war, the territories were divided and the country of Iraq was created despite having Sunni Muslims, Shiite Muslims, and Kurds in the north. Many of these different sects wanted independence right from the start.

After British rule ended and the country was granted its independence, it became a republic—in name only. In truth, the country was taken over by strongman dictators for years until the US-led invasion under President George W. Bush led to the ousting of tyrant Saddam Hussein. After that, Iraqis approved their own constitution and elected a 275-member Council of Representatives of Iraq. In 2006, the country celebrated its first constitutional government in almost fifty years.

While Hussein's tyranny and crimes against his own people are not questioned, his extreme tactics did keep terrorists and extremism out of his country. Since his departure, the overwhelming majority of Christians living in the country fled to neighboring nations out of fear of Islamic fundamentalists.[5]

Since 2015, the country's military—mainly trained by American forces—have had to battle terrorists from ISIS, who have taken over large amounts of territory throughout the country.

The fear is that Iraq may become a hotbed for extremism and terror, just as Afghanistan was under the Taliban rule.

Israel has long been a point of contention between the Arab world and Americans. You also have to consider that the United States has historically backed leaders who were very unpopular with their own citizens, such as the shah of Iran, whose overthrow and exile led to the Iranian hostage crisis in 1979 where American embassy workers were held in captivity and threatened with death for 444 days.

In fact, the shah—Mohammed Reza Pahlavi—was being ousted by a fledgling democratic government when the CIA helped bring about a military coup that restored his power. But he was eventually overthrown and exiled. The United States over the years even backed Saddam Hussein for a time as well as Libyan strongman Muammar Gaddafi, despite their atrocities and support of terrorist actions.

Maybe it's just a case of preferring to deal with the dictator you know rather than the unknown. These uneasy alliances have never been as complicated and tested as the US alliance with the region's richest and perhaps most influential country: Saudi Arabia.

Saudi Arabia is ruled by an oil-rich monarchy, and strict religious laws are enforced. For example, homosexuality is illegal as is playing of musical instruments in public. There are public floggings and executions. Drugs are not tolerated and those caught with drugs—especially foreigners—are often executed, according to the CIA World Factbook.

Saudi Arabia's Role

There is also growing evidence that Saudi Arabia's government plays both sides of the conflicts brought about the terror problem and have been accused as state sponsors of

Iraqi dictator Saddam Hussein is shown here protesting the guilty verdict at his trial. He was later hanged by Iraqi authorities.

terrorist activities. Osama bin Laden was a Saudi national and even today, the majority of ISIS fighters are from Saudi Arabia.

But the most damaging information of all are reports from US intelligence agencies that Saudi Arabia had ties to the 9/11 hijackers and their operations. This has caused outrage among many Americans, including families of those who lost their lives on 9/11.[6] It would lead to an eventual showdown between Obama and Congress that

Origin of "Terrorism" and "Terrorist"

It's interesting to note that the first use of the term "terrorism" in the English language can be traced back to actions of a legitimate government. In 1795, the rulers of France employed harsh and deadly tactics—including mass executions by way of the guillotine—to terrorize its own citizens into submission.

The origins of terror can be traced back to ancient times when the Zealots of Judea carried out clandestine assassinations and murders of Roman soldiers who were occupying their land. Much later, many barbarian-type armies utilized fear and terror by being particularly vicious and gruesome in their warfare and tactics.[7]

But the modern-day origin of the terrorist can be found in Russian nationalists, Irish separatists, and Palestinians protesting the creation of Israel after World War II.

The inspiration for the rise of these groups was due to several factors, including nationalism, anti-colonial resentments, and sometimes just new ideologies. For example, the Irish Republican Army was created by Irish Catholics who wanted independent rule and felt oppressed by protestant Great Britain.

Continued on page 68

Continued from page 67

In the late 1960s, terror groups began to hijack airplanes to terrorize, often trading the planes for cash or the release of some of their imprisoned members. It would be forty years later that terrorists would once again hijack planes, but this time they would fly them into buildings instead of attempting some sort of negotiation.

Terror groups operated within the United States as well. Groups like "The Weathermen" would plant bombs and try to create hysteria to protest America's involvement in the Vietnam War.[8]

could have repercussions for years to come in the war on terrorism.

But before the president had to deal specifically with that confrontation, it was ISIS, along with instability in Iraq and the entire Arab world, that would command most of his attention. The war on terror would now have more moving pieces and more layers than ever.

CHAPTER

SEVEN

SYRIA

> **❝The threat from terrorism is real,
> but we will overcome it.❞**
>
> —*Barack Obama, December 6, 2015*

When American troops left Iraq in 2011, President Obama and his advisers had long known about the insurgent terrorist group known as ISIS, or Islamic State.

But they had also believed the group to was already defeated. In fact, five years earlier the US military conducted operations to find and kill the leader of the Iraq insurgency believed to have been the leader of ISIS as well.

They were so sure that the threat had been neutralized that they even lowered the amount of the bounty or reward leading to the death or capture of the group's new leader from $5 million to only $100,000.[1]

But only a few months after American troops were gone from Iraq, the group began to flourish. The group had set up a stronghold in Iraq but was now going over the border into Syria as well. Remember, the Iraqi border was created after World War I and the Islamic State did not recognize it now. They were actually creating their own country or state. Syria was in the midst of a bloody civil war and it was easy for the group to gain a foothold amid the chaos.

American intelligence agencies were gathering information quickly but there were so many pieces at play. The Arab Spring, a series of anti-government protests, uprisings, and armed rebellions across the Middle East around 2011, resulted in feel-good stories for a while but also resulted in more instability in the already-volatile region.

In 2012, a report by the US Defense Intelligence Agency to President Obama warned that the chaos in Iraq and Syria could allow the group to grow stronger. The report said ISIS could "declare an Islamic state through its union with other terrorist organizations in Iraq and Syria."[2]

President Obama took a cautious approach. The last thing he wanted to do was send American soldiers back to the region to fight yet another new enemy. He also said that ISIS was really just an extension of previous terror groups and blamed the previous administration's decision to invade Iraq in the first place. Plus American forces were working with a multi-national force put together to combat terror in the region.

"ISIS is a direct outgrowth of al-Qaeda in Iraq that grew out of our invasion," he said. "Which is an example of unintended consequences. Which is why we should generally aim before we shoot. We've got a sixty-country coalition. We will slowly push back ISIS out of Iraq. I'm confident that will happen."[3]

Also, many believed that the group was so brutal, so violent, and so terrible that perhaps the group would implode. After all, they were conducting mass beheadings

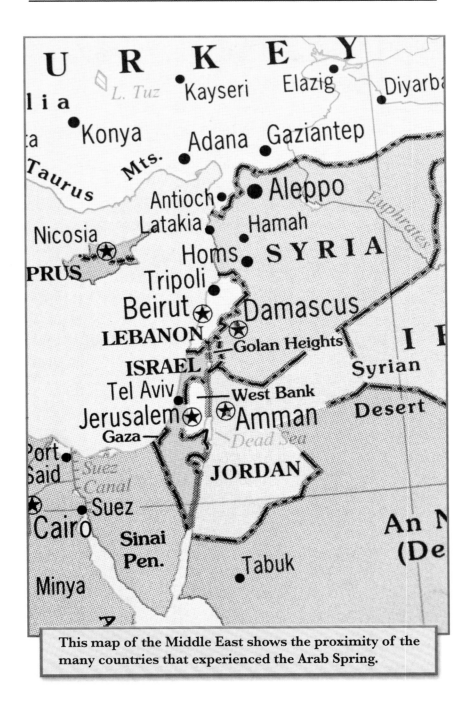

This map of the Middle East shows the proximity of the many countries that experienced the Arab Spring.

Muammar Gaddafi

One of the more historical and significant events resulting from the Arab Spring was the death of Col. Muammar Gaddafi, the longtime dictator of Libya.

Gaddafi was a hero to his people when, as a captain in the military in 1969, he led a bloodless coup to overthrow the government and seize power for himself. He was young, charismatic, and handsome, and the people loved that he was sick and tired of foreign oil companies dictating the price of oil. Since Libya had a vast number of oil reserves, he felt foreigners were keeping his country poor.[4]

Gaddafi was born in 1942 to nomadic parents. He received no formal education other than the teachings in the Koran and whatever education he received as part of his military training. Yet, he rose to power and he successfully renegotiated oil deals so that Libya would reap part of the profits. It was a great victory for him.

He soon grew to think of himself as a great political philosopher and enacted harsh laws. He was not tolerant of any views other than his own, and it wasn't long until the promising young revolutionary became a ruthless dictator bent on maintaining his power at any cost.

In the years that followed, his behavior became more erratic. He dressed in outlandish and colorful outfits and spewed anti-American rhetoric. In 1986, he was believed to have ordered the bombing of a club in Berlin, Germany, where many American soldiers were. The US president at the time, Ronald Reagan, called him the "Mad Dog of the Middle East" and ordered American planes to bomb Libya in retaliation.[5]

Libyan dictator Muammar Gaddafi became an erratic leader over the years and was an open supporter of terrorism.

Gaddafi was later found responsible for the Libyan terrorist bombing of a Scottish airliner that killed two hundred seventy-nine people.

During the Libyan revolution, Gaddafi went into hiding. He was found in a culvert by revolutionaries who dragged him through the street and killed him.

as well as kidnapping young girls from areas where they had power and used them as sex slaves.

"There was a strong belief that brutal insurgencies fail," said William McCants, an expert on ISIS. "The concept was that if you just leave the Islamic State alone, it would destroy itself, and so you didn't need to do much."[6]

Al-Qaeda vs. ISIS

So, what's the difference between al-Qaeda and ISIS? Well, though both organizations use terror as a means to an end, the brutality of ISIS is far more barbaric than that of al-Qaeda. That may be hard to believe but al-Qaeda officials have criticized ISIS in the past for the number of beheadings they perform.[7]

But the main difference between the groups is that ISIS sees itself as one day becoming a legitimate state, a country with a government and infrastructure. The goals of al-Qaeda were to spread Islam, instill fear, and force Westerners from Arab lands.

The real turning point in the rise of ISIS was when Iraq's neighbor, Syria, erupted into a bloody civil war. That uprising from Syria's citizens was another offshoot of the phenomenon known as the Arab Spring.

What to Do About the Growing Threat

For President Obama, part of the challenge he faced in dealing with the growing threat of ISIS was that Americans were battle-weary and not very enthusiastic about committing more soldiers and military resources toward another bloody campaign. Even as the civil war in Syria became

Arab Spring

On December 17, 2010, something happened in the small African country of Tunisia that would send shockwaves throughout the Middle East and the Arab world for years to come. It would also greatly affect President Obama's war on terror.

Tired of living under dictatorships, human rights violations, poverty, and corrupt leadership, the people

Continued on page 76

President Barack Obama addresses the American people on television regarding the war in Iraq.

Continued from page 75

of Tunisia and several Arab countries seemed ripe for revolution. Tunisian labor unions, facing harsh and unsafe work conditions, decided to hold walk-outs, strikes, and other non-violent labor practices.

This type of behavior was almost unheard of. Immediately, word of these acts spread through the use of social media, mainly Facebook and Twitter. Similar occurrences began taking place in Algeria and Egypt.

People started demonstrating, wanting a voice in the government. They filled the plazas and public squares of their cities. Despite the respective governments ordering the military to take action, the demonstrations were kept mainly peaceful.

The president of Tunisia fled to Saudi Arabia while the president of Egypt resigned. Democratic countries, including the United States we,re said to be aiding in the peaceful revolutions.

Of course, not all the Arab Spring rebellions were bloodless. In Libya, for example, longtime leader Muammar Gaddafi was ousted from power and then executed. The country—along with Syria, Yemen, and Iraq—remains embroiled in civil war as different factions fight to seize power.

Tunisia's revolution ended with a democracy in place. Other pushes for freedom did not go as well. The unrest and civil wars in Syria and Iraq became a fertile breeding ground for terror.

more violent and forced Russia to get involved, the president was reluctant to act.

He said the Americans stood with the Syrian people in solidarity but would not commit to sending troops there.

"For us to get entangled in Syria is a serious step, and we have to do so making absolutely certain who we are helping and we're not putting arms in the hands of folks who could eventually turn them against us or our allies in the region," the president said in 2012.[8] Of course he was referring to America's experience with backing Osama bin Laden in Afghanistan's war against the Soviet Union.

But ISIS would continue to grow and even create a *caliphate,* or a capital, in Iraq, led by prophets who receive their power directly from the Islamic prophet Muhammad himself.

But, the president would eventually have to do something, as images of terror were now being broadcast on American televisions almost daily. The ISIS propaganda machine began ramping up efforts to recruit disillusioned or disenfranchised Muslims from Western society. They would target these individuals and indoctrinate them into their ideology and then turn them into full-fledged terrorists.

Knowing they could not go up in battle against military forces from the United States or its allies, ISIS leaders began a terror campaign aided by social media that not only sent fear around the globe but was as shocking as anything many had ever seen.

ISIS started to kidnap any Westerner who crossed its path. That included journalists, aid workers, Christian missionaries, and even medical personnel there in the region to assist the victims of war. The group would make outlandish demands in exchange for its hostages, knowing the demands would never be met. That led to the inevitable.

In August 2014, ISIS videotaped and broadcast the beheading execution of American journalist James Foley. The freelance journalist, who worked for several different news organizations, had traveled to Libya to cover the uprising against Gaddafi. Instead, he became the first American citizen killed by ISIS. The brutal video shocked Americans.

President Obama had to calm a distraught and scared country. He went on television to condemn the execution

An Iraqi man rides his bicycle past a billboard that proclaims support for ISIS.

and promised the American people that ISIS and its legacy of terror would be defeated.

"They have rampaged across cities and villages killing innocent, unarmed civilians in cowardly acts of violence," Obama said. "They abduct women and children and subject them to torture and rape and slavery. They have murdered Muslims, both Sunni and Shia, by the thousands. They target Christians and religious minorities, driving them from their homes, murdering them when they can, for no other reason than they practice a different religion."[9]

It would prove easier said than done.

CHAPTER EIGHT

TERROR GOES
DOMESTIC

“I have made it clear that we will
hunt down terrorists who threaten
our country, wherever they are. That
means I will not hesitate to take
action against ISIL in Syria, as well
as Iraq. This is a core principle of my
presidency: if you threaten America,
you will find no safe haven.”

—*Barack Obama, on the anniversary of
the 9/11 attacks, September 11, 2014*

After the 9/11 attacks in 2001, the American government
started several domestic operations to monitor some of its
own citizens. The programs were controversial, as many
people believed them to violate civil liberties. However, the
programs were ultimately successful.

Although there were no attacks on American soil for many years, there were a few random attacks by Americans who had become radicalized or brainwashed by terrorist ideology. The worst was in 2009 when a Muslim, Nidal Hasan, serving as a major in the US Army, opened fire on his comrades at Fort Hood, Texas, where he was stationed. He killed thirteen and injured another thirty-three.

Before the shootings, Hasan communicated with a radical Islamic leader and switched allegiances from the US military to the Taliban.[1] He was captured and tried by the military for thirteen counts of premediated murder for which he was found guilty and sentenced to death.

President Obama was criticized by many for refusing to categorize the murders as terrorism for many years. He described the events as tragic but classified the attacks as a case of workplace violence. This was despite a US Senate committee on homeland security calling it the worst terror attack on the United States since 9/11. A *Washington Times* editorial even described the president's refusal to call the murders terrorist in nature a "denial."[2]

This was a big deal at the time because the soldiers murdered and injured by Hasan were not eligible to receive the Purple Heart medal for being injured by an enemy combatant. It also restricted the kind of medical coverage and financial restitution Hasan's victims could receive. It wasn't until 2015 that the president called Hasan's attack as an act of terror.[3]

A few years after being sentenced to death, it was learned that Hasan was in communication with ISIS leaders. He wrote them a letter asking to be admitted as a member of ISIS.

FBI Failure?

According to numerous reports, the actions of US army major and psychiatrist Nidal Hasan in the months leading up to his murder of thirteen were warning signs that were taken very seriously.

Hasan's sometimes erratic behavior as he entered the world of radicalized Islam made him the focus of an FBI investigation. So, why did the FBI conclude there was nothing to worry about shortly before Hasan opened fire on his peers in 2009?

The FBI is continuously updating its list of the most wanted terrorists in the world.

Hasan had become agitated and seemingly anti-United States in the months before the shootings. He began communicating with a radicalized Muslim cleric in Yemen and even expressed support for suicide bombers.

When questioned by authorities, Hasan said the emails were being conducted as a part of his research into terror groups for his work as an army psychiatrist. But when more red flags surfaced, the FBI was reluctant to take the investigation further.[4] Critics called the FBI's inaction as "political correctness gone too far."

Reports said that Hasan had started getting into arguments with fellow soldiers about the US war on terror. He also began sharing anti-American sentiments with anyone who would listen. But the FBI defended its actions by saying that at the time there seemed to be no credible threat of violence from Hasan.

Anwar al-Awlaki, a radical Muslim cleric living in Yemen who was corresponding with Hasan, took to his English-language website the day following the attacks and praised Hasan as a hero.

The FBI would come under fire again a few years later after another man they investigated for terrorist ties killed dozens in a nightclub.

"It would be an honor for any believer to be an obedient citizen soldier," Hasan wrote in the letter.[5]

Unfortunately for American citizens and a president fighting seemingly endless wars in Afghanistan and other areas against terror, the Fort Hood "lone wolf" attack was only the beginning.

Lone Wolves and Small Cells

Was Hasan guided or ordered to kill? That remains uncertain. But what is certain is that lone wolf operators or small cells began their terror campaigns over the next few years in Western countries around the world. No one would feel their sting like two countries in particular: France and the United States.

A 2012 shooting in France claimed multiple lives and was attributed to ISIS. But it was an event on American soil a year later that really shocked the world.

On April 15, 2013, at about 2:50 in the afternoon, two bombs exploded within twelve seconds of each other near the finish line of the annual Boston Marathon. The blast killed three and seriously wounded 264.

The bombs, containing BBs and pellets, were inside pressure cookers, hidden inside backpacks. The attacks and aftermath were caught on television, bringing the reality of terror right into everyone's living rooms.

The president had to respond quickly, not knowing yet whether this was indeed an act of terror. A few hours after the blast, he went on television to reassure the American people.

Boston police officers scramble as they assist the injured and look for suspects moments after two bombs exploded at the 2013 Boston Marathon.

"We will find out who did this. We'll find out why they did this. Any responsible individuals, any responsible groups, will feel the full weight of justice."[6]

Surveillance video and tips allowed the police to identify the bombers as a pair of Muslim brothers who immigrated legally to the United States from Chechnya—twenty-six-year-old Tamerlan Tsarnaev and nineten-year-old Dzhokhar Tsarnaev.

The following night, the brothers were involved in a shootout with police. One officer died, and so did Tamerlan Tsarnaev. His younger brother would be captured four days after the bombing after an all-out manhunt and door-to-door search of the neighborhood they believed he had fled to.

It was revealed during the trial that the brothers were interested in jihadist propaganda videos and radical Islamic beliefs as far back as 2012. Like Hasan, the brothers began sympathizing with Islamic fighters and terrorists and would often say things like the victims of bombings were of no importance because they were nonbelievers.[7]

The brothers told friends that they found most of the information that led to their radicalization on the internet. That gave President Obama and his cabinet yet another platform or front where they would have to start waging war with terrorists, including ISIS (also called ISIL by President Obama to refer to more widespread terrorist groups in the Middle East): the internet.

"As we know all too well, terrorist groups like ISIL have called on people around the world and here in the United States to attack innocent civilians. Their propaganda, their videos, their postings are pervasive and more easily

Propaganda

To put it simply, "propaganda" is basically the term used to purposely manipulate someone for your own political purposes. It is a way to persuade someone to your way of thinking. The tactic has been used in just about every modern war. But it is not relegated solely to wartime.

In the 1930s, the Nazi movement in Germany began a propaganda campaign against the Jewish population of the country. The idea was to turn the majority of the population against the Jewish minority. This, of course, led to the Holocaust, where six million Jews were murdered. In the years leading up to the Holocaust, Jews were depicted as rodents or bugs on posters and flyers. They were shown as rich and greedy people whose mere presence was bad for the country. Since the country was mired in an economic depression, the people were eager for someone to blame.

By the time the Holocaust began, the mindset of many was that Jews were not people but vermin—like rats and bugs—that needed to be eliminated.

In the war against terror, ISIS and other terror groups have used propaganda to inspire attacks on Westerners and even to recruit. And these are not just posters and flyers.

In fact, ISIS has a media wing known as Al Hayat that has produced hundreds of films, ranging from three-minute beheading videos to hour-long features. Their films are part history and part travel documentary, and they feature atrocities as well. The films are said to have high production value and even utilize special effects.[8]

accessible than we want," he would later say. "As I've said before, these lone actors or small cells of terrorists are very hard to detect and very hard to prevent. But across our government, at every level—federal, state, and local, military and civilian—we are doing everything in our power to stop these kinds of attacks."[9]

But really, what could be done to stop individuals bent on destroying society as we know it? And how do you win a war on the internet against fanatical groups who target the disenfranchised, the lonely, the bullied, and the poor?

Strategies for Stopping Terror Recruitment

Over the next few years, President Obama's White House staff would work to try to figure out a strategy that worked against the highly successful online recruiting initiated by ISIS and other terrorist organizations. Over the course of many years they would try everything from a graphic, violent online video to a Disney film.

One effort that came under fire by critics was the use of English-language websites and videos to counter those produced and posted in cyberspace by ISIS. Other efforts to slow down internet recruiting efforts by terrorists were seen as too tame.

Finally, the president's staff decided to try an approach that was more in line with what ISIS was actually doing. A video, "Run to ISIS Land" was produced and nearly went viral.

The video, meant to mimic and satire an ISIS recruiting video, starts out by encouraging believers to "Run, do not walk, to ISIS Land." Then the video goes on about new skills to learn like "crucifying and executing Muslims." The video then shows numerous ISIS atrocities, such as kneeling prisoners being shot point-blank; severed heads positioned next to a propped-up corpse; limp bodies left hanging from crosses in public squares.[10]

Even though this new video was gruesome and was blasted by critics, it seemed to get under the skin of ISIS leaders and spread the message that the organization was nothing but a dirty abomination of Islam.[11]

THE POWER OF WORDS

> **❝We need not throw away 200 years of American jurisprudence while we fight terrorism. We need not choose between our most deeply held values, and keeping this nation safe.❞**
>
> —*Barack Obama*

One of President Obama's tools against the threat of terrorism from radical Muslim jihadists came in the power of words. It was not in the form of propaganda or angry speeches. It was not even in the form of the words he used. It was more the words he chose not to use.

This made some Americans angry, but Obama had a plan. He refused to use the words "radical Islam" to describe the attacks on American citizens. His reason? With more than a billion Muslims in the world, the president's strategy was simple. He did not want to paint the entire Muslim world with one brushstroke for fear of alienating the Muslim population and perhaps feeding the notion that ISIS was trying to propagate—that the Western world hated Islam.

The terror strategy had changed now as well. Instead of attacking such high-profile targets as the World Trade Center or the Pentagon, terrorists decided to go after "soft" targets or places where no one would expect an attack and where security would not be tight.

The pressure on Obama and his administration to use the term "radical Islam," or that the Western world—the United States in particular—was at war with radical Islam grew as more and more attacks took place.

More Attacks

On November 13, 2015, terrorists—including some who entered France under refugee status—conducted coordinated attacks throughout Paris, killing 137 people and wounding 368.

The horrific attacks could have actually produced more carnage as gunmen opened fire in the middle of a rock concert. A few miles away, bombs exploded at a packed soccer stadium during an international match between the national teams of France and Germany. Nearby, gunmen opened fire at a crowded café. The bombs did not do the damage or kill people the way the terrorists had hoped.

Paris was truly a scene of horror and of war. In fact, it was the worst attack on French soil since World War II.

Only three weeks later, a married couple in California, Rizwan Farook and Tashfeen Malik, shot and killed fourteen people and injured twenty-two more at a San Bernardino community center during what was supposed

French soldiers prepare to raid an apartment as they hunt for the terrorists behind the Paris terrorist attack of 2015.

to be an office Christmas party. The couple were later shot and killed in a shootout with police.

The pressure mounted on the president to say the United States was at war with Islam. If he didn't say it, his critics argued, it seemed as if radical Islam was at war with the United States.

A little more than six months later it happened again.

During the early morning hours of June 12, a radicalized Muslim entered a gay nightclub in Orlando, Florida, and started firing. He also called 911 and told authorities that he was a member of ISIS. The shooter, Omar Mateen, was born in the United States to parents from Afghanistan.

Mateen became radicalized in the years leading up to the shooting and was even investigated by the FBI for statements he supposedly made about being a terrorist. The FBI investigated him twice but eventually cleared him when they found no credible threat. But the threat was there. When American forces dropped bombs in Iraq that killed Abu Wahib—an ISIS leader—weeks earlier, Mateen decided to act.

He walked into the gay nightclub armed with a handgun and automatic rifle. He started firing, trapping many in corners and in bathrooms. Eventually he was shot and killed by police. When it was all said and done, Mateen

Thousands of people gather in Orlando, Florida, for a candlelight vigil to honor those killed at the Pulse Nightclub terror attack of 2016.

killed forty-nine people that night, making him the worst mass murderer in American history.

There were reports that Mateen was driven by hatred of homosexuality, which is strictly forbidden in the Islamic faith. But other reports insisted that he frequented the club in the past.[1]

Whatever the motivation, again President Obama cautioned against using the term "radical Islam." He even chastised his critics in a speech shortly after the deadly attack.

"And let me make a final point," the president said. "For a while now, the main contribution of some of my friends on the other side of the aisle have made in the fight against ISIL is to criticize this administration and me for not using the phrase "radical Islam." That's the key, they tell us—we can't beat ISIL unless we call them 'radical Islamists.' What exactly would using this label accomplish? What exactly would it change? Would it make ISIL less committed to trying to kill Americans? Would it bring in more allies? Is there a military strategy that is served by this? The answer is none of the above. Calling a threat by a different name does not make it go away. This is a political distraction. Since before I was president, I've been clear about how extremist groups have perverted Islam to justify terrorism. As president, I have repeatedly called on our Muslim friends and allies at home and around the world to work with us to reject this twisted interpretation of one of the world's great religions.

Homegrown Terror

As groups like ISIS ramp up propaganda and recruiting efforts, they will continue to find and successfully recruit Americans willing to switch allegiances from their home country to the country or region of their ancestors.

Omar Mateen is the perfect example.

Born in Queens, New York, to Afghan parents, Mateen moved with them to a well-to-do neighborhood in Port St. Lucie, Florida. The family seemed to assimilate well into American culture. But things began to slowly change when the United States became involved in a war in Afghanistan after the 9/11 attacks.[2]

Mateen started acting out in school as his father became more agitated by the war. He would talk of violence and sex. As he grew older he was known as always being agitated and angry.

He was known for making inappropriate jokes, often involving guns and violence. He also was unlucky in pursuing his goal of becoming a police officer. He was in training to become a corrections officer but was terminated for sleeping in class and for making inappropriate comments about violence.[3]

The FBI investigated him a second time after it was revealed that he had been friendly with a man from his mosque in Fort Pierce, Florida, who carried out a suicide bombing in Syria.

Perhaps the biggest challenge for President Obama and his administration was the difficulty in detecting and stopping people like Mateen, who did not seem to have any direct contact with or training from a terrorist organization. They instead act out on their own while pledging allegiance to the terror cause.

The FBI has said it is conducting 900 investigations of suspected Islamist militants in the United States.[4]

President Barack Obama looks troubled just before he addresses the media regarding the war on terror and the term "radical Islam."

"So there's no magic to the phrase 'radical Islam.' It's a political talking point; it's not a strategy. And the reason I am careful about how I describe this threat has nothing to do with political correctness and everything to do with actually defeating extremism. Groups like ISIL and al-Qaeda want to make this war a war between Islam and America, or between Islam and the West. They want to claim that they are the true leaders of over a billion Muslims around the world who reject their crazy notions. They want us to validate them by implying that they speak for those billion-plus people; that they speak for Islam. That's their propaganda. That's how they recruit. And if we fall into the trap of painting all Muslims with a broad brush and imply that we are at war with an entire religion— then we're doing the terrorists' work for them."[5]

Making Some Headway

During that same speech, the president outlined some advancements made against ISIS, especially by way of trying to share their power base and actual land that their forces occupy. He would be relying heavily on his secretary of defense, Ash Carter, who took over the position in 2015.

The American aircraft carrier USS *Harry S. Truman* has been part of the US Navy's efforts to fight the war on terror since the first days of the war.

Ash Carter

Ashton B. Carter is the United States' twenty-fifth secretary of defense. He was born on Sept. 24, 1954, in Philadelphia, Pennsylvania. He was nominated to the position by President Obama, replacing Chuck Hagel in the position in 2015. A brilliant man and physicist by trade, Carter studied at Yale, Oxford University as a Rhodes Scholar, and Massachusetts Institute of Technology. Later he taught at Harvard University.

Beginning in the 1990s, Carter began serving in one capacity or another at the Department of Defense, where his background as a physicist was useful when it came to nuclear weapons, among other topics.

Despite differing with Obama on several of the president's policies, such as negotiating with Iran, releasing prisoners held at Guantanamo Bay, and how much support to give Ukraine in its conflict with Russia, the secretary of defense was very much on board with the president regarding the threat of ISIS and the need to destroy the organization.

During a speech in 2016, Carter compared ISIS to a form of cancer.

"Our coalition's military campaign plan, as you all know, has three objectives," he told a group of representatives from countries who have allied itself with the United States against ISIS. "The first is to destroy ISIL's parent tumor in Iraq and Syria. That's necessary, but it's not sufficient. As recent attacks in our homelands remind us, ISIL's safe havens threaten not only the lives of the Iraqi and Syrian people, but also the security of our citizens in other countries. And the sooner we defeat ISIL in Iraq and Syria, the safer our countries will be.

So we have a second objective also, which is to combat ISIL's metastases everywhere they emerge around the world. And we have a third and very important mission, which is to help protect our homeland, along with law enforcement and intelligence officials."[6]

The president said that the military was ramping up the number of bombs being dropped on ISIS's stronghold, from B-52 bombers that were taking off from the US aircraft carrier *Harry S. Truman* in the Mediterranean Sea. He said there were 13,000 bombing runs producing favorable results, including killing more than 150 top ISIS leaders.

Obama also said that the strategy was to continue chipping away at the land being controlled by the terrorists in both Iraq and Syria. Another way to hurt the group, he said, was to take away its main source of funding by destroying or taking over oil fields.

"Cutting off ISIL's money may not be as dramatic as military strikes, but it is critically important," Obama said of the strategy. "And we're seeing the results. ISIL's cash reserves are down. It has had to cut salaries for its fighters. It's resorting to more extortion of those trapped in its grip. And by ISIL's own admission, some of its own leaders have been caught stealing cash and gold. Once again, ISIL's true nature has been revealed: These are not religious warriors, they are thugs and they are thieves."[7]

CHAPTER

TEN

WHAT'S NEXT?

> **❝**I know that after so much war, many Americans are asking whether we are confronted by a cancer that has no immediate cure.**❞**
>
> —*Barack Obama, December 6, 2015*

The future of the United States and the war on terrorism was a prevalent theme all throughout 2016 with one of the most contentious and divisive presidential campaigns in the country's history. Both candidates—Hillary Clinton and Donald Trump—played up the importance of stopping the ISIS threat and keeping Americans safe.

Their ideas were different. While Obama and Clinton stressed gun control and trying to ban assault weapons in order to keep them from potential terrorists, Trump focused his thoughts on doing a better job at vetting immigrants from countries that have been hotbeds of terror.

Putting Boots on the Ground

But even as President Obama chastised the nation for criticizing his refusal to say "radical Islam" and as the final days of the presidential campaign were winding down, he was working on a plan to neutralize the ISIS threat.

The president, his military advisers, top generals, and leaders from coalition forces had been working hard devising a strategy for a ground offensive against the Iraqi and Syrian ISIS headquarters. The attacks began in early October and no one believed it would be easy.

After all, for example, ISIS had control of Iraq's second largest city—Mosul—for almost two years without any

Presidential hopefuls Donald Trump and Hillary Clinton shake hands before a 2016 debate. Trump went on to defeat Clinton and succeed Obama as president.

military opposition. The same can be said for the ISIS capital of Raqqa, located in civil-war torn Syria.

Defense Secretary Ash Carter called the attacks a "decisive moment" in the effort to finally defeat ISIS.[1] Leaders did warn however that the battles could last for months.

During the weeks leading up to the battle in Mosul, Kurdish troops trained by American and Iraqi forces, surrounded ISIS military bases in and around Mosul in order to keep the ISIS members from fleeing the region and resurfacing in nearby Syria.

Nearly 4,000 Kurdish troops started the battle by taking control of several small villages in the region that had been under ISIS control. American Special Operations commandos, in Iraq to train the forces, would join the battle once it got underway.

The operation became a source of nationalism and pride for Iraq's prime minister Haider al-Abadi, who vowed to unite Iraq once again.

"The Iraqi flag will be raised in the middle of Mosul, and in each village and corner very soon," he told his citizens during a televised announcement of the attacks.[2]

Carter, while warning that the battles would be costly and certainly not won overnight, said they were necessary in order to protect the world from the threat of terrorism.

"The fight will not be easy and there is hard work ahead, but it is necessary to end the fiction of ISIL's caliphate and disrupt the group's ability to carry out terror attacks against the United States, our allies, and our partners," Carter said. "The international coalition will continue to do what we can to enable local forces in both Iraq and Syria to deliver ISIL the lasting defeat it deserves."[3]

In October 2016, Americans supported Iraqi forces as they led an all-out offensive to liberate the city of Mosul from ISIS occupation.

Fighting a war against an opponent that relies on terror and chooses to blend in with its surroundings rather than field a traditional military force in uniforms is difficult. There needs to be great care taken not to harm civilians but at the same time not allow the enemy to flourish and continue their deadly deeds. That being said, there is an enormous amount of pressure on the president to show the American people that progress is being made. And that necessitates a certain amount of information being released to the public.

When President Obama announced that ISIS strong-holds were being attacked, he was roundly criticized by

The President's Cabinet

You've heard the term "cabinet" before when hearing or reading about politics. You probably know that the term refers to some of the president's top advisers. But who exactly is in the cabinet and where did the term come from?

The idea of a cabinet was established in Article II, Section 2 of the Constitution to advise the president on any matter that he or she seeks counsel.

The cabinet has been in existence since George Washington became the first president of the United States. It includes the vice president and the heads of fifteen executive departments—the secretaries of agriculture, commerce, defense, education, energy, health and human services, homeland security, housing and urban development, interior, justice, labor, state, transportation, treasury, and veterans affairs—as well as the attorney general.[4]

Cabinet members typically serve one term if a president is re-elected and President Obama's presidency was no different.

Arguably the most important cabinet position and certainly one of the most respected positions of public office in the world is the secretary of state. During Obama's war on terror, he counted heavily on Hillary Clinton, and then John Kerry, who served as secretary of state.

Since the war on terror started, the positions of secretary of defense and the secretary of homeland security have taken on more importance and more responsibility as they work toward keeping Americans safe.

incoming president Donald Trump, who defeated former secretary of state and first lady Hillary Clinton in the 2016 presidential election.

Throughout his sometimes controversial campaign, Trump complained that Obama often gave the enemy too much information. The attack on Mosul was no exception.

"Whatever happened to the element of surprise, right?" Trump said to a group of supporters at a campaign rally only days before he was elected president. "What a group of losers we have. And now it's a very tough battle, they're dug in. It's a very—much tougher than they thought. We need different thinking in this country, folks. They should have kept their mouths shut."[5]

A Long Way to Go

And while it is true that the battle did bog down and prog-ress was achieved very slowly for US-backed forces, Trump's comments were believed to be overstated. The truth is that ISIS had two years to hunker down and make Mosul a tough place for their enemies to recapture. The battle to free Mosul from the grip of terror continues into Trump's presidency.

A few weeks after the battle began, ISIS launched a strong counterattack against Iraqi and coalition forces, mainly through the use of long-range artillery, suicide bombers, and the despicable use of citizens forced to become human shields.

"(They) have continued to hide behind civilians and facilitate harm to them," said Colonel John Dorrian, a spokesman for the US-led coalition, which aided the Iraqi attacks by providing air strikes. But he did say that the

President Donald Trump

History—actually, stunning political history—was made on November 8, 2016, when New York businessman and former reality television star Donald Trump stunned the world by defeating former secretary of state and former first lady Hillary Clinton to become president of the United States.

Trump, who rose to prominence as a real estate tycoon, appealed to the middle class of the country, calling them the forgotten men and women. He rode their enthusiasm to victory.

But the war on terror was also a huge reason why Trump was elected. With the increasing attacks taking place on American soil in Orlando, Boston, and San Bernadino, Trump campaigned on a platform of being tougher on terror and immigration, and he disagreed with how President Obama waged the war on terrorism. Immigration—especially undocumented immigration across the relatively unsecured border with Mexico as well as the potential influx of immigrants from war-torn areas in Iraq and Syria—was also a lynchpin issue for Trump as he campaigned. Trump pointed to the fact that some of the terrorists who participated in the deadly attacks in Paris entered France as refugees from Syria.

Lastly, Trump disagreed with Obama's policies regarding the downsizing of the military, saying that he wanted to rebuild a strong and mobile force that might be able to serve as a deterrent around the world.

Trump's campaign was controversial mainly because of his outspoken nature, including making comments that some said were offensive, racist, and sexist.

A big part of Obama's legacy will relate to the war on terror. This 2017 photo was taken during his last press conference. Soon the war would be the responsibility of Donald Trump.

plan to retake Mosul was developed with the notion of reducing "the possibility of civilian casualties and collateral damage."[6]

By early November 2016, there were some that were already praising the attack and calling it the beginning of the end for ISIS. Jan Kubris, the United Nations envoy for Iraq, said steady progress was being made and that it would be important to make sure the region was stabilized once the enemy was defeated.[7]

President Obama inherited a war that started before he took office and continues after he left office in January 2017. Only time will tell whether his policies had a lasting effect or whether he should have done something else.

But the sad truth is that the United States, and much of the Western world, will be fighting a war against terrorism for some time to come.

CONCLUSION

There is no real conclusion that can be made because the war on terrorism continues. It began before President Obama took over as president of the United States and continues after he left office after eight years.

The war was brought to the United States on Sept. 11, 2001, and has ebbed and flowed since then. What can we conclude about President Obama's war on terror?

Well, he will long be remembered as the president who brought 9/11 mastermind and al-Qaeda leader Osama bin Laden to justice during a daring overnight mission carried out by Seal Team Six.

He will also be remembered for following through on his promise to end the war in Iraq and bring the troops home from such a bloody, costly, and unpopular war. For those accomplishments he will likely always be praised.

Of course, his critics would argue that he ordered troops to abandon Iraq prematurely and that resulted in the rise of ISIS. Critics would also point to the fact there are still

The sixteenth President of the United States, Abraham Lincoln, is known for his presidency during the Civil War, which resulted in the end of slavery in the United States.

prisoners being held at Guantanamo Bay, something he vowed to end during his first presidential campaign.

The truth is that President Obama was an antiwar candidate, pledging to end the wars he inherited from the Bush administration. But the reality is that he spent more time as a wartime president than Franklin D. Roosevelt, Lyndon B. Johnson, Richard M. Nixon, or Abraham Lincoln.[1]

And that was the quandary that he faced throughout his eight years. He did not want to be at war, but he knew it was necessary. Both his critics and his supporters will say he never allowed the wars to take his attention away from other important matters facing the country like health care, the economy, and education.

"No president wants to be a war president," said Eliot A. Cohen, a military historian at Johns Hopkins University. "Obama thinks of war as an instrument he has to use very reluctantly. But we're waging these long, rather strange wars. We're killing lots of people. We're taking casualties."[2]

Whether you conclude that President Obama was successful or not while waging the war on terror, one thing cannot be disputed. President Obama stuck to his guns and never allowed himself to paint the war on terror as a war with Islam. He remained respectful of the religion and those who practice it. He remained steadfast that human rights and caring for refugees far outweigh the fear of terror.

Lastly, he never allowed Americans to feel as if they must cower in fear or alter their daily routines for fear of terrorism. Only time will judge the president's actions and whether or not he was successful.

CHRONOLOGY

September 11, 2001

Terrorists hijack several American passenger jets and crash them into the World Trade Center, the Pentagon, and a field in Pennsylvania, killing 2,993 people.

September 20, 2001

The phrase "war on terror" is officially used.

October 7, 2001

The United States invades Afghanistan as part of Operation Enduring Freedom.

October 26, 2001

Congress passes the controversial Patriot Act, broadening the power of the American government to spy on its own people in order to prevent terror attacks.

January 2002

A detention camp for captured members of the Taliban or al-Qaeda is opened by the United States at a naval base in Guantanamo Bay, Cuba.

March 20, 2003

Calling it central to the war on terror, President George W. Bush orders the invasion of Iraq.

2004

With the use of drones and intelligence gathered by the CIA, the United States conducts anti-terror operations in numerous countries.

November 5, 2006

After being previously captured by American forces, Iraq dictator Saddam Hussein is hanged by Iraqi authorities.

November 4, 2008

Barack Obama is elected the forty-fourth US president and the first African American president.

August 2009

The Obama administration changed the phrase "war on terror" to "war with al-Qaeda."

May 2, 2011

Osama bin Laden, mastermind of the 9/11 attacks, is shot and killed by American forces in Pakistan.

December 18, 2011

American forces leave Iraq, thus ending the war.

September 11, 2012

Islamic militants attack the American embassy in Benghazi, Libya, killing four Americans.

June 13, 2014

The terrorists, having regrouped under the name ISIS and taken over many regions of Iraq, force President Obama to order military personnel to return.

September 22, 2014

American military operations against ISIS begin in Syria.

January 1, 2015

Another American war in Afghanistan begins.

January 7, 2015

Terrorists kill more than a dozen workers at a French magazine in Paris.

November 13, 2015

Terrorists kill 139 during several attack in Paris.

December 2, 2015

A married couple with ties to radical Islam and ISIS, kills twenty-two people attending a Christmas party in San Bernadino, California.

March 22, 2016

Terrorists kill thirty-nine during a bombing in Brussels.

June 12, 2016

An Afghan American, swearing allegiance to ISIS, kills forty-nine people at a nightclub in Orlando, Florida.

July 14, 2016

A terrorist kills eighty-four people in Nice, France.

October 2016

American forces support massive operations in Mosul, Iraq, and Raqqa, Syria, to remove ISIS from power.

CHAPTER NOTES

INTRODUCTION

1. "9/11 Attacks," History.com, http://www.history.com/topics/9-11-attacks.
2. George W. Bush "9/11 Address to the Nation," Sept. 11, 2001. americanrhetoric.com, http://www.americanrhetoric.com/speeches/gwbush911addresstothenation.htm.

CHAPTER 1. HUMBLE BEGINNINGS

1. Barack Obama. *Dreams from my Father* (New York, NY: Random House Books, 1995), p. 37.
2. Associated Press. "Obama Wins Senate Race to Become 5th Black U.S. Senator in History." Nov. 2, 2004. http://usatoday30.usatoday.com/news/politicselections/vote2004/2004-11-02-il-ussenate_x.htm (accessed August 16, 2016).
3. Barack Obama. *Keynote Address at the Democratic National Convention on July 27, 2004 in Boston.* https://www.youtube.com/watch?v=eWynt87PaJ0 (accessed September 7, 2016).

CHAPTER 2. A WAR INHERITED

1. Missy Ryan. "The Guantanamo Quagmire: Still No Trial in Sight for 9/11 Suspects." *Washington Post*, Sept. 6, 2016. https://www.washingtonpost.com/world/national-security/no-end-in-sight-for-troubled-guantanamo-trials-once-seen-as-a-swift-path-to-justice/2016/09/06/b7833b5a-704a-11e6-8533-6b0b0ded0253_story.html (accessed September 8, 2016).
2. Justin Sink. "Obama Remains Hopeful of Closing Guantanamo Bay Before His Term Ends." *Bloomberg*, September 8, 2016. http://www.bloomberg.com/politics/articles/2016-09-08/obama-remains-hopeful-of-closing-guantanamo-bay-before-term-ends (accessed September 8, 2016).
3. Charles Babington and Michael Abramowitz. "U.S. Shifts Policy on Geneva Conventions." *Washington Post*, July 12, 2006. http://www.washingtonpost.com/wp-dyn/content/article/2006/07/11/AR2006071100094.html (accessed September 9, 2016).
4. Peter Baker and Thom Shanker. "Obama Plans to Retain Gates at Defense Department." *New York Times,* November 25, 2008. http://

www.nytimes.com/2008/11/26/us/politics/26gates.html?_r=0 (accessed September 9, 2016).

5. Ibid.

6. Mark Thompson. "The Pros and Cons of Keeping Robert Gates." *Time*, November 21, 2008. http://content.time.com/time/nation/article/0,8599,1861038,00.html (accessed September 9, 2016).

7. Katie Rooney. "Closing Gitmo, Restarting Diplomacy." *Time*, April 28, 2009. http://content.time.com/time/specials/packages/article/0,28804,1889908_1889909_1893203,00.html (accessed September 12, 2016).

8. Ibid.

9. Jim Miklaszewski. "First 100 days: Obama's Approach to Two Wars." NBCnews.com, April 28, 2009. http://www.nbcnews.com/id/30458191/ns/politics-white_house/#.V9_cM_krLIU (accessed September 12, 2016).

CHAPTER 3. SHIFTING THE FOCUS

1. Jim Miklaszewski. "First 100 days: Obama's Approach to Two Wars." NBCnews.com, April 28, 2009. http://www.nbcnews.com/id/30458191/ns/politics-white_house/#.V9_cM_krLIU (accessed September 12, 2016).

2. Ibid.

3. Tamara Cofman Wittes. "The Slipperiest Slope of Them All." *The Atlantic*. March 12, 2016. http://www.theatlantic.com/international/archive/2016/03/obama-doctrine-goldberg-inaction/473520/ (accessed September 15, 2016).

4. National Counterterrorism Guide. "al-Qaeda." https://www.nctc.gov/site/groups/al_qaida.html (accessed September 15, 2016).

5. Ibid.

6. Jessica Stern. "Obama and Terrorism: Like It or Not, the War Continues." *Foreign Affairs*. September/October 2015. https://www.foreignaffairs.com/articles/obama-and-terrorism (accessed September 15, 2016).

7. John McCain. "Sen. McCain press release." May 27, 2014. http://www.mccain.senate.gov/public/index.cfm/press-releases?ID=de23d2f5-3704-4e71-bffd-57396b52527b (accessed September 15, 2016).

8. Michael O'Brien. "Republicans Criticize Obama over Iraq Withdrawal." NBC News. October, 21, 2011. http://firstread.nbcnews.com/_news/2011/10/21/8433344-republicans-criticize-obama-over-iraq-withdrawal (accessed September 15, 2016).

CHAPTER 4. MANHUNT

1. Kate Zernike and Michael T. Kaufman. "The Most Wanted Face of Terrorism." *New York Times*. May 2, 2011. http://www.nytimes.com/2011/05/02/world/02osama-bin-laden-obituary.html?_r=0 (accessed September 20, 2016).
2. Ibid.
3. Ibid.
4. Special Report: The End of bin Laden. *Time*. May 20, 2011. http://content.time.com/time/magazine/0,9263,760111 0520,00.html (accessed September 820 2016).
5. Peter Bergen. "A Long Time Going." *Time*. May 20, 2011.http://content.time.com/time/magazine/article/0,9171,2069610,00.html (accessed September 20, 2016).
6. Staff Report. "Who Are the Taliban." BBC News. May 26, 2016. http://www.bbc.com/news/world-south-asia-11451718 (accessed September 23, 2016)
7. Ibid
8. Special Report: The End of bin Laden.
9. Ibid.

CHAPTER 5. KILLING BIN LADEN

1. Macon Phillips. "Osama bin Laden Dead." Official White House press release. May 2, 2011. https://www.whitehouse.gov/blog/2011/05/02/osama-bin-laden-dead (accessed September 23, 2016).
2. Ibid.
3. Chris Megerian. "Americans Rejoice After Long Awaited Death of Osama bin Laden." NJ.com. May 2, 2011. http://www.nj.com/news/index.ssf/2011/05/americans_both_celebrate_and_r.html (accessed September 25, 2016).
4. Phillips.
5. Mark Mazzetti, Nicholas Kulish, Christopher Drew, Serge F. Kovaleski, Sean D. Naylor, and John Ismay. "Seal Team 6: A Secret

History of Quiet Killing and Blurred Lines." *New York Times*. June 6, 2015. http://www.nytimes.com/2015/06/07/world/asia/the-secret-history-of-seal-team-6.html?_r=0 (accessed September 15, 2016).

6. Ibid.

7. Ibid.

8. Nicole Gaouette. "Five Years Ago the U.S. Killed Osama bin Laden. Did It Matter?" CNN. May 2, 2016. http://www.cnn.com/2016/05/02/politics/terrorism-bin-laden-raid-2016-isis/ (accessed September 23, 2016).

9. Ibid.

10. Lauren Walker. "Panetta's Memoir blasts Obama on His Leadership, Blames Him for the State of Iraq and Syria." *Newsweek*. October 10, 2014. http://www.newsweek.com/panettas-memoir-blasts-obama-his-leadership-blames-him-state-iraq-and-syria-276582 (accessed September 26, 2016).

11. Ibid.

CHAPTER 6. **THE RISE OF ISIS**

1. Tamara Cofman Wittes. "The Slipperiest Slope of Them All." *The Atlantic*. March 12, 2016. http://www.theatlantic.com/international/archive/2016/03/obama-doctrine-goldberg-inaction/473520/ (accessed September 15, 2016).

2. Matt Compton. "President Obama Has Ended the War in Iraq." The White House official press release. Oct. 21, 2011. https://www.whitehouse.gov/blog/2011/10/21/president-obama-has-ended-war-iraq (accessed September 26, 2016).

3. Brian Montopoli. "Obama Announces End of Iraq War, Troops to Return Home by the End of the Year." CBS News. Oct. 21, 2011. http://www.cbsnews.com/news/obama-announces-end-of-iraq-war-troops-to-return-home-by-year-end/ (accessed September 24, 2016).

4. Middle East Police Council. "Maliki's Actions Continue to Antagonize Sunni Muslims." Middle East in Focus. May 2016. http://www.mepc.org/articles-commentary/commentary/malikis-actions-continue-antagonize-iraqi-sunnis?print (accessed September 26, 2016).

5. Central Intelligence Agency. "Iraq." The World Factbook. https://www.cia.gov/library/publications/the-world-factbook/geos/iz.html (accessed September 26, 2016).

6. Gregory Korte. "Why Obama doesn't wants 9/11 families suing Saudi Arabia." USA Today Newspaper. Sept. 24, 2016. http://www.usatoday.com/story/news/politics/2016/09/23/obama-veto-terrorism-lawsuit-bill-setting-up-override-battle/90407496/ (accessed October 2, 2016).

7. Terrorism Research. "The History of Terrorism." Terrorismresearch.com http://www.terrorism-research.com/history/early.php (accessed September 26, 2016).

8. About News. "The History of Terrorism." Aboutnews.com. http://terrorism.about.com/od/whatisterroris1/p/Terrorism.htm (accessed September 30, 2016).

CHAPTER 7. SYRIA

1. Ian Fisher. "In Rise of ISIS, No Single Missed Key But Many Strands of Blame." *New York Times*. Nov. 18, 2015. http://www.nytimes.com/2015/11/19/world/middleeast/in-rise-of-isis-no-single-missed-key-but-many-strands-of-blame.html (accessed October 2, 2016).

2. Ibid.

3. Heather Saul. "President Obama Claims Rise of ISIS Is Unintended Consequence of George W. Bush's Invasion of Iraq." *The Independent.* March 18, 2015. http://www.independent.co.uk/news/world/middle-east/president-obama-claims-rise-of-isis-is-unintended-consequence-of-george-w-bush-s-invasion-in-iraq-10115243.html (accessed October 2, 2016).

4. Martin Asser. "The Muammar Gadaffi Story." BBC News. Oct. 21, 2011. http://www.bbc.com/news/world-africa-12688033 (accessed October 2, 2016).

5. Ibid.

6. Fisher.

7. Ibid.

8. Michael Kaplain. "Obama's War on ISIS 2016: Quotes Showing President's Evolution on Syrian Civil War." *International Business Times*. April 25, 2016. http://www.ibtimes.com/obamas-war-

isis-2016-quotes-showing-presidents-evolution-syrian-civil-war-video-2359190 (accessed October 2, 2016).

9. Barack Obama. "White House Statement." Aug. 20, 2014. https://www.whitehouse.gov/the-press-office/2014/08/20/statement-president (accessed October 6, 2016).

CHAPTER 8. **TERROR GOES DOMESTIC**

1. Molly Hennessey-Fiske. "From Death Row, Ft. Hood Shooter Requests to Join Islamic State." *Los Angeles Times*. Aug. 30, 2014. http://www.latimes.com/nation/nationnow/la-na-nn-fort-hood-shooter-islamic-state-20140830-story.html (accessed October 6, 2016).

2. Patrick Goodenough. "Six years Later: Obama Finally Calls Fort Hood a Terrorist Attack." CNS News. Dec. 7, 2015. http://www.cnsnews.com/news/article/patrick-goodenough/obama-six-years-later-calls-fort-hood-terrorist-attack (accessed October 6, 2016).

3. Ibid.

4. CBS News/AP. "Lawmaker: Reports Shows FBI Iignored Accused Fort Hood Shooter Nidal Hasan Out of Political Correctness." CBS News. July 19, 2012. http://www.cbsnews.com/news/lawmaker-report-shows-fbi-ignored-accused-fort-hood-shooter-nidal-hasan-out-of-political-correctness/(accessed October 6, 2016).

5. Hennessey-Fiske.

6. CNN Library. "Boston Marathon Terror Attack Fast Facts." CNN.com. April 18, 2016. http://www.cnn.com/2013/06/03/us/boston-marathon-terror-attack-fast-facts/(accessed October 20, 2016).

7. Hilary Sargent. "The Radicalization of Tamerlan Tsarnaev." *Boston Globe*. April 28, 2015. https://www.boston.com/news/local-news/2015/04/28/the-radicalization-of-tamerlan-tsarnaev (accessed October 20, 2016).

8. Simon Cottee. "Why It's So Hard to Stop ISIS Propaganda?" *The Atlantic*. March 2, 2015. http://www.theatlantic.com/international/archive/2015/03/why-its-so-hard-to-stop-isis-propaganda/386216/ (accessed October 10, 2016).

9. Barack Obama. "Remarks by the President After Counter-ISIL meeting." The White House. June 14, 2016. https://www.

whitehouse.gov/the-press-office/2016/06/14/remarks-president-after-counter-isil-meeting (accessed October 20, 2016).

10. Greg Miller and Scott Higham. "In a Propaganda War Against ISIS, the U.S. Tried to Play by the Enemy's Rules." *Washington Post.* May 8, 2015. https://www.washingtonpost.com/world/national-security/in-a-propaganda-war-us-tried-to-play-by-the-enemys-rules/2015/05/08/6eb6b732-e52f-11e4-81ea-0649268f729e_story.html?tid=a_inl (accessed October 20, 2016).

11. Ibid.

CHAPTER 9. THE POWER OF WORDS

1. Alan Blinder, Jack Healey, and Richard A. Oppel. "Omar Mateen: From Early Promise to F.B.I. Surveillance." *New York Times.* June 12, 2016. http://www.nytimes.com/2016/06/13/us/omar-mateen-early-signs-of-promise-then-abuse-and-suspected-terrorist-ties.html (accessed October 20, 2016).

2. Dan Barry, Serge Kovaleski, Alan Blinder, and Mujib Mashal. "Always Agitated. Always Mad: Omar Mateen, According to Those Who Knew Him." *New York Times.* June 18, 2016. http://www.nytimes.com/2016/06/19/us/omar-mateen-gunman-orlando-shooting.html?rref=collection%2Fnewseventcollection%2F2016-orlando-shooting&action=click&contentCollection=us&region=rank&module=package&version=highlights&contentPlacement=1&pgtype=collection (accessed October 22, 2016).

3. Ibid.

4. Peter Bergen. "The Real Terror Threat in America Is Homegrown." CNN. June 13, 2016. http://www.cnn.com/2016/06/12/opinions/orlando-homegrown-terror-bergen/ (accessed October 22, 2016).

5. Barack Obama. "Remarks by the President After Counter-ISIL Meeting." The White House. June 14, 2016. https://www.whitehouse.gov/the-press-office/2016/06/14/remarks-president-after-counter-isil-meeting (accessed October 22, 2016).

6. Ash Carter. "Opening Remarks at Counter-ISIL Defense Minister Meeting." July 20, 2016. http://www.defense.gov/News/Speeches/Speech-View/Article/850519/opening-remarks-at-counter-isil-defense-minister-meeting (accessed October 24, 2016).

7. Obama.

CHAPTER 10. **WHAT'S NEXT?**

1. Michael R. Gordon and Tim Arango. "East of Mosul, Kurdish Troops Advance on ISIS-held Villages." *New York Times*. Oct. 17, 2016. http://www.nytimes.com/2016/10/17/world/middleeast/iraq-isis-mosul-battle.html (accessed November 6, 2016).

2. Ibid.

3. Ash Carter. "Statement by Secretary of Defense Ash Carter on Raqqa." Nov. 6, 2016. http://www.defense.gov/News/News-Releases/News-Release-View/Article/997338/statement-by-secretary-of-defense-ash-carter-on-raqqa (accessed November 6, 2016).

4. White House. "The Cabinet." https://www.whitehouse.gov/administration/cabinet (accessed November 6, 2016).

5. Jeremy Diamond. "Trump Continues to Knock Mosul Offensive." CNN.com Nov. 7, 2016. http://www.cnn.com/2016/11/05/politics/donald-trump-mosul/index.html (accessed November 7, 2016).

6. Associated Press. "ISIS Counterattacks Show Tough Battle Ahead for Mosul City Center." CBS News. http://www.cbsnews.com/news/isis-counterattacks-in-the-center-of-mosul/(accessed November 7, 2016).

7. Associated Press. "Mosul Operation Is the Beginning of the End: UN." CBS News. http://www.cbsnews.com/news/mosul-operation-is-the-beginning-of-the-end-of-isis-u-n-says/

CONCLUSION

1. Mark Landler. "For Obama, an Unexpected Legacy of Two Full Terms at War." *New York Times*. May 14, 2016. http://www.nytimes.com/2016/05/15/us/politics/obama-as-wartime-president-has-wrestled-with-protecting-nation-and-troops.html (accessed October 28, 2016).

2. Ibid.

GLOSSARY

agonized Having a hard time, suffering.

allegiance To be loyal to a country or a cause.

coalition An alliance of different countries, usually only temporary.

continental Being attached to a continent.

crucial Of the utmost importance.

disarray In shambles and not organized.

interrogation A non-friendly or adversarial way of getting information from someone, usually a prisoner.

legitimate Something that is lawful or legal.

mastermind The person who devises an idea and follows up on making sure it is carried out.

neutralize To make something ineffective or harmless.

nomination The person who has been chosen to run for office.

radicalized To believe in an extreme or distorted version of something.

rebellion Resisting or acting out against the government or authority.

unprecedented Something that has never happened before.

weary Tired of dealing with the same problem or issue over and over.

FURTHER READING

BOOKS

Duffy, Helen. *The War on Terror and the Framework of International La w.* Cambridge, UK: Cambridge University Press, 2015.

Maraniss, David. *Barack Obama: The Story.* New York, NY: Simon & Schuster, 2012.

Obama, Barack. *After Osama Bin Laden: America's New Counter-Terrorism Strategy.* Beijing, China: Intercultural Publishing, 2011.

Washington Post. State of Terror: The War on ISIS. Washington, DC: Diversion Books (e-book), 2015.

WEBSITES

Barack Obama
barackobama.com
Put together by Organizing for Action, this site discusses creating positive, long-lasting change.

Global Issues: War on Terror
globalissues.org/issue/245/war-on-terror
Social, political, and economic analysis of the war on terror

Global Policy Forum
globalpolicy.org/war-on-terrorism.html
A think tank's detailed record and opinion of the war on terror

The White House
whitehouse.gov
News, views, and stances taken by the American president

VIDEOS

"Osama Bin Laden: War on Terror."
2016, Directed by Janson Media.

"Where Were You: Events that Changed the World."
2010, Directed by Janson Media.

INDEX